Here, There and Everywhere

Lindsey Jane Doley

Here, There and Everywhere

Memoirs of an Air Hostess

Author's note
Most of the names of people in this book have been changed.

Here, There and Everywhere: Memoirs of an Air Hostess
ISBN 978 1 76041 718 5
Copyright © Lindsey Jane Doley 2019

First published 2019 by
GINNINDERRA PRESS
PO Box 3461 Port Adelaide 5015
www.ginninderrapress.com.au

Contents

1	Around the World in Maths Class	9
2	Fast Forward	13
3	Training Wheels – I Mean Wings	16
4	Hostesses Must Not – Crazy Coffee Service	20
5	All the Pretty Aeroplane Ladies in Their Technicolor Uniforms	24
6	Market Day in Mount Gambier	27
7	Do You Remember?	30
8	Fond Memories of Old Airports	34
9	Terrorism	37
10	Leerers and Lechers	39
11	'Doing the Continental'	45
12	Grasse Romeo	48
13	Waterloo	51
14	Green Eggs and Tehran	53
15	No Room in Geneva	57
16	Herr Pfaffenbichler	62
17	First Class All the Way	67
18	The Case of the Lost Coats in the Sacks of Potatoes	71
19	Robbed in Brussels	76
20	Jump on Those Scales and Ping That Girdle	80
21	Not For Sale, Ever	83
22	Sometimes It's Just the Little Things, Part 1	84
23	Sometimes It's Just the Little Things, Part 2	88
24	Things on Planes That Go Bump in the Night	93
25	Coming to America and Canada Too	96
26	Oregon With Ryllis and Charlie	99
27	Postcards from America	103
28	Sunny San Francisco	106

29	Indiana	110
30	Toronto	113
31	Back to the Wild, Wild West	117
32	'Uh, Oh, We're In Trouble'	120
33	In Praise of Ploughman's Lunches and Peter Rabbit	123
34	New Zealand, My Narnia: South Island	126
35	Sometimes It's Just the Little Things: At Home and Overseas	134
36	New Zealand, My Narnia: North Island	141
37	Now for Something Completely Out of Sequence, Part 1	149
38	Now For Something Completely Out of Sequence, Part 2	152
39	All Roads Lead to Stockholm	155
40	And Then Back To London	159
41	Grand Finale, Part 1	165
42	Grand Finale, Part 2, With a Sting at the End of the Tale	175

I dedicate this book to my husband John and to all the air crew – both pilots and hostesses– and passengers I flew with throughout my eleven years with Ansett Airlines of South Australia.

1

Around the World in Maths Class

I've always loved travel and aircraft, but I'm not sure exactly when I picked up the bug. I think it began in earnest when I was about seven and Mum, Dad and I went on holidays to Melbourne. We spent two leisurely days driving there and overnighted in lovely grand-looking old hotels along the way: the kind with huge staircases and a beautifully shiny, copper gong on the ground floor to summon guests to breakfast. Today, most of these buildings are National Trust listed and, if they're still functioning as hotels or even backpacker lodges, prices have risen accordingly. For me, the chance to visit another state and see different scenery, towns and people was terribly adventurous and exciting. You'd have thought I'd been to London, instead of Victoria, the state next door.

Then, in 1960 at age nine, Mum, Dad, my nanna and I all took off on holidays again, this time to Sydney. This was partly a working holiday for my dad, as the company he worked for had their head office in Sydney. This time around was a camping trip. I was in seventh heaven and, yes, I loved camping back then. I thought our large hired tent was wonderful and, at that age, it seemed almost the size of a circus tent. I remember my dad practising pitching it on our lawn and I'd spend a delightful afternoon playing in it. Once on the road, I'd look forward to every late afternoon when Mum and Dad would drive into a camping ground to pitch our tent. Of course the adults did all the hard work, while I was free to trot off merrily to the playground; there was just about always a good one, sometimes with other children to talk to. My favourite piece of playground equipment was the swings.

I'd swing as high as I could, within my own safety limits, and pretend I was flying, a free sensation I loved. Then I'd return to the nearby tent for tea and a sleep. How I enjoyed sleeping on a stretcher bed in that tent, along with Mum, Dad and my nanna, even though she snored a bit.

These days, camping would have to take the form of glamping which, for those who are unfamiliar with this term, means camping done in style and comfort. Others do the hard work, while the guests just get to look good, smell nice and see interesting places. Nowadays I've decided I do rather like my creature comforts and I'm unwilling to go without showers or to prepare a meal at the end of a long day's drive. However, I imagine a glamping holiday would be quite expensive, because of course you have to pay for the pleasure of being catered to.

One day, while in Sydney, my mum and dad took me to see the international Kingsford-Smith Airport at Botany Bay. It was impressive to me back then, but you should see it now, it's massive. A Qantas Boeing 707 was sitting out on the tarmac, all sleek and silvery in the sun, waiting to take off to San Francisco in far-away America. The Boeing 707 was a state-of-the-art long-haul aircraft at the time; I guess it was the 1960s version of an A380. I was mesmerised and thought I'd never seen anything so beautiful or magnificent. I can recall being tangibly jealous of passengers who were heading out across the tarmac to board the plane; so I decided then and there that, one day, it would definitely be me.

Back at school in Adelaide, I'd become travel and aeroplane mad. In arithmetic classes, which I hated with a passion at school, I'd pull my atlas onto my knees under the desk and try to look at it furtively, mentally planning all the trips I was determined to take one day. San Francisco and London topped off my list, and I'd daydream of flying in a Boeing 707 just like the one I'd seen in Sydney. Of course, my inattention was discovered by my teacher on more than one occasion and I was in trouble, with some sort of imposition to be done after school, such as 'I will not gaze at my atlas in arithmetic class' fifty

Boeing 707, Frankfurt airport.

times. It might have been, but I can't remember and I don't think I cared very much. I have since thought that seeing the streamlined 707 in Sydney that day sowed a tiny seed of inspiration which was to grow and develop into the early 1970s, when my dreams of flying as a career came to fruition.

I loved to watch aircraft, whether in the air or on the ground. I can remember often pestering Mum and Dad to take a weekend drive to Adelaide's West Beach Airport, so that I could walk out onto the windblown observation deck and gaze at aircraft, hear their noisy engines rev up, both props and jets at that time, and smell the avgas, which I think must have been flowing in my veins even then. It's so sad that this experience isn't available today.

I was ecstatic when, in 1964, I'd been staying on Kangaroo Island for a week of the May school holidays. I'd spent a pleasant week with my aunt, uncle and cousins. My nanna was there too. The icing on the cake for me, however, was the chance I had to fly back to Adelaide with Nanna, who had booked a flight in preference to the ferry, as she knew how much I'd love it. We flew in a Convair 440 with Airlines of South Australia. The Convairs were wonderful aircraft. They seated about fifty-two passengers and apparently even had a family compartment, although I wasn't aware of that. Many of the older AASA hostesses who I later flew with enjoyed relating their experiences on the Convair 440.

Apparently they even used to fly up to Hayman Island wearing special tropical dresses for working in the cabin.

Anyway, on the Kangaroo Island to Adelaide flight, I had a window seat and was offered some lollies, but I don't seem to remember either of the two air hostesses doing a mad dash with a coffee service as I did later, in 1973. It was a smooth flight and we landed at sunset. I relived that flight for weeks afterwards and I think even then my head was firmly in the clouds. Perhaps that was the moment that I thought, this is for me. That moment came in the early 1970s.

I've wondered since whether there's some truth to visualisation, as my dodgy under-the-desk travels eventually materialised and I've been fortunate enough to visit New Zealand, in a Qantas 707, no less; London and Europe multiple times; and the USA and Canada twice. Even after I'd left the airlines, I added Bali, Singapore, Penang to my list and lovely New Zealand twice more. I have marvellous memories of going here, there and everywhere.

2

Fast Forward

Fast forward now to 1971. I'd made up my mind about the career I wanted to pursue. On a cold, brisk morning at Sydney's Mascot Airport (the domestic terminal), I was descending the steps of an Ansett Airlines of Australia Boeing 727, my hair and my long purple paisley print 1970s scarf blowing wildly in the stiff breeze. I was in Sydney for a holiday with some relatives and I remember wearing a purple velvet mini dress and white patent knee-high boots, which were very trendy at the time. I thought I was pretty groovy; typical twenty-year-old thinking. Does anyone remember the word groovy? It was one of the buzzwords of the time, almost every second word in the *Brady Bunch*, if you ever watched it.

Anyhow, there I was at Sydney airport. I may have literally come down to earth, but my head was well and truly back in the clouds, imagining myself in the Ansett uniform, doing the cabin demo and practising saying, 'Would you like tea or coffee?'

I thought I would be just perfect for the job and at that moment I realised I wanted it like nothing else.

Fast forward again, this time to 1973; after two interviews with Ansett Airlines of South Australia (AASA) management and a newly acquired St John Ambulance first aid certificate, wave your magic wand and hey presto, there was I in the uniform of Ansett Airlines of South Australia, which was a subsidiary company of Ansett. Also operating at the time were Ansett Airlines of New South Wales and McRobertson Miller Airlines in Western Australia. I had decided to join the smaller subsidiary company to make sure, I suppose, that I enjoyed flying as a

One of the photos included in my application to join AASA.

job. I was pretty sure I would, but joining the larger mainline company would have meant an upheaval to Melbourne for training and then to goodness knows where in Australia. I put joining the big company on the back-burner for the time being.

One advantage with AASA was that the crew were able to be back in Adelaide, our base, every night, except for unpredictable weather or a breakdown, which was a possibility you always had to be prepared for. At the time I was still living at home with my mum, dad and sister, so for now, that situation suited me.

My AASA uniform was a lovely raspberry colour, which suited my dark hair, but I did have a funny little hat with a sort of tassel in the middle of the crown. My mum called it my monkey hat. Gee, thanks, Mum. We also had to wear gloves for boarding passengers and disembarkation. How times have changed. Hat and gloves sounds so very 60s.

A few weeks before joining AASA, I took a two-week coach tour of New Zealand. This had been a trip I was scheduled to do about a month later but, because of my acceptance with the airlines, my travel agent did some quick fancy footwork and found me an earlier tour. This was my very first overseas trip and guess what? I flew in a Qantas Boeing 707, just like the one I'd seen years before at Kingsford Smith. No passports were required for New Zealand at the time if you were Australian. Hard to believe now, isn't it? I discovered the joy of duty-free shopping and was over-awed at the array of glamorous, shiny goods on offer. I remember well purchasing a French perfume; Princesse d' Albret, by Jean d'Albret. I still have the empty bottle and amazingly it has retained a haunting smell of the original contents. The perfume doesn't seem to have deteriorated much with age. I don't know whether they make them like that any more. I also bought two silky long-sleeved tops.

I had a rip-roaring time on both the South and North Islands, revelling in the astounding scenery, the company of some other young people on the tour and discovering New Zealand ice cream, as well as spending up in the shops of almost every town I visited.

The day after my return, I began my training with Ansett Airlines of South Australia. On my first day, I caught a suburban bus to the airport from the city and alighted just beside the West Beach Airport gates. I then walked into the terminal building in my pale blue suede shoes (thank goodness it wasn't raining), to match my pale blue angora dress, and was quite surprised at the distance, which seemed so quick when in a car. I wasn't driving at that stage. I also hadn't realised that I could have hopped on an Ansett airport bus which departed from the Ansett office situated on North Terrace. I wasn't yet a seasoned or savvy traveller, but definitely young, enthusiastic and more than a little naïve.

The stories that follow are from those exhausting, happy, frustrating, turbulent (in more ways than one) days. Although there will be many hostess stories, I also want to portray travel as it was in the 1970s and 1980s, as well as revisit attitudes in society, fashions (fun and fabulous) and music (also fun and fabulous) when the world in my opinion was a bit more peaceful and travel was simpler and more pleasant as a result.

3

Training Wheels – I Mean Wings

Training at Airlines of South Australia was intense. I'd been prepared for a certain amount of study, but this was like being in the final year of high school. Still, I found it all interesting and wanted to do well, so I put my head down and really focused.

Training period consisted of three weeks' ground training in a small room next to the hostess lounge and five weeks of in-flight training. We studied safety procedures, which are always of paramount importance for any airline, first aid (I already had a mandatory St John Ambulance certificate) and of course uniform regulations and grooming. We were soon to discover the joys to come of on-the-spot grooming checks.

Every day after the nine-to-five school, there was more study to do at home. As it was winter and often cold and wet, and it seemed particularly so that year, I used to sit in bed after tea and read through what we'd learned that day, for a test the following day. A grade of ninety per cent or more was expected from these tests, so it was a good thing I really wanted this and found it fascinating

I didn't have much of a social life during training. I wasn't dating anyone at the time, which was perhaps just as well. I had friends of my age (twenty-two), but many of them had already partnered off and married, so our lives were taking us in different directions. I have no regrets whatsoever that I chose my direction. In the 70s it was still quite common, indeed almost expected, that girls would marry at age twenty or twenty-one. The old-maid stigma was rife for any girl not married with a couple of kids by twenty-five.

My company on a Saturday night was K.C. Kasem's *American Top*

On my first day of flight training, in raspberry-colour uniform with navy blue shoes and bag.

Forty, which I loved. You may remember listening to KC. I can still remember listening and dancing around my room to many of my favourites: Suzi Quatro, Paul McCartney and Wings, Paul Simon, Australia's Helen Reddy, and Deep Purple; and the list goes on. Lately I've been listening to some of K.C. Kasem's 1973 programmes on YouTube for a nostalgia trip.

Following the three weeks of intense ground training came five weeks of equally intense in-flight training. This all happened in the aircraft favoured by ASA: the Fokker Friendship, or F27. These noisy little blighters were turboprops and sat forty to forty-four passengers. This sounds small but there was still plenty of scope for things to go wrong or people to be demanding. I wished that ASA had still operated the DC3 and Convairs which they'd had until 1972, but I was doing my dream job and didn't mind too much. We also finally had a uniform and a flight trainer. Mine was a very pretty blonde girl called Noeline. She was friendly and easy to get along with, but also firm when necessary. She was perfect for me. Noeline had just returned from her honeymoon. It was only in early 1973, or it could have been 1972, that legislation was passed allowing air hostesses to continue flying once they were married.

I ended up with plenty of blisters on my feet and bruises on my legs and arms. Of course I hadn't yet found my flying feet (balance) and so I'd get knocked around a fair bit if it was on a rough flight.

Our routes consisted of Adelaide to Kangaroo Island, to Port Lincoln (dubbed Stinkin' Lincoln), then from Port Lincoln on to Ceduna on the west coast of South Australia on Mondays and Thursdays. Also, Adelaide to Whyalla, to Broken Hill and to Woomera, where there was a rocket range and military staff. Woomera was an all-day trip: up there in the morning, with a quick stop at Edinburgh air force base en route, then the day spent at the mess and back in the late afternoon. There wasn't a great deal to do at Woomera, but there was a plant nursery and I remember visiting that and buying a pretty red hibiscus plant for my mum. She had it for ages, and maybe still has. I must ask sometime.

A year or so later, Mount Gambier in the south-eastern part of our state was included on our route map. This was a favourite flight with all the girls; we only had girl cabin crew at this time, as it too was an all-dayer. We were given a room in one of the nicer hotels in Mount Gambier and we'd go shopping. Mount Gambier was, and still is, a large, bustling country town and almost on the South Australian/Victorian border. Because of its relatively close proximity to Melbourne, the boutiques in Mount Gambier were always stocked with the more sophisticated clothes from cosmopolitan Melbourne; at least we thought they were and we often brought back additions to our wardrobes. Mount Gambier is also known for its famous Blue Lake, which is the remains of an old volcano. I'd always thought the volcanoes in the south-east were extinct, but recently I read where given the right circumstances, they could roar back to life again. Eek!

Mount Gambier was a favourite destination with everyone, I think. It had so much to offer. There are cave systems there, some of which you could visit with a guide, and sinkholes and a rich dairy industry. Later I'll tell you about the cheese and sausage specials which developed out of our Mount Gambier flights.

Training finally finished; it was spring now and the sun came out. I was awarded my lovely little wing badge, which I still have. I was now known as Hostess Westcott, which is my maiden name. A year or so later, I became better known as LJ by most airport staff; a friendly sort of nickname which stuck until my final day in December 1984. I'd successfully passed my exams and training, and was off and away and excited about all the possibilities that flying offered.

4

Hostesses Must Not – Crazy Coffee Service

Hostesses must not read, knit, sew, eat sweets or chew gum in uniform. Neither must they swear (as if) or discuss religion or politics (likewise as if). So said the *Air Hostess Manual* of the early 70s and most likely 50s and 60s too. I wonder what's in today's manuals? Although the above sounds rather stuffy, I must admit that seeing an air hostess doing any of those things would not be a good look. I once boarded an American Airlines plane back in 1975 and there was an air hostess standing in the aisle chewing gum quite obviously. Later in the flight, the same girl, when asked by a passenger what kind of alcoholic drinks they stocked on board, replied carelessly, 'Geez, we probably got any kinda booze ya want.' I remember not being terribly impressed with her manner.

Also, air hostesses were not allowed to display affection in public. Preferably, air hostesses should be superhuman, which is a feat we managed sometimes.

Being superhuman reminds me of the coffee service we provided on the Kangaroo Island flights. Kangaroo Island is situated at the lower end of St Vincent's Gulf in South Australia and is a favourite tourist destination. Google it; it's a lovely place and only thirty minutes by plane from Adelaide. These days, our coffee service would defy all occupational health and safety regulations. It was insane. Here's what we'd have to do in about twenty minutes.

We'd fill a large and quite heavy tray with rows of cups and airline plates, complete with serviettes, sugar, spoons and rows of Ansett biscuits. We'd then have to pick up this tray and rest it on the seat tops, while asking people if they wanted coffee. Of course everyone said yes

Fortieth anniversary coaster used in cabin service in 1976.

and some even wanted tea, but that wasn't available. We'd then have to hold the laden tray with one hand and quickly – time was definitely of the essence here – make up the small airline tray, with a cup, spoon, sugar and biscuits to give to the passenger with the other hand.

Before starting this service, you'd have to remember to offer the people in the front row a pillow on which to rest their tray, as there were no tables fitted there. Even before that, you'd have to have served the pilots first and get given the estimated time of arrival (ETA) and a weather forecast, which was very relevant to KI flights.

Anyway, there we would be, doing our juggling act, moving up the rows and going from side to side. The other hostess came behind, carrying a jug of very hot coffee in one hand and a milk jug in the other, so she had no spare hand to hold onto anything in the event of turbulence. Neither did the girl holding the tray for that matter. The KI flights were quite bumpy most of the time, because, being of short duration, the plane flew at a fairly low altitude: about 6,000 to 7,000 feet. In winter, conditions were worse, with more rain and wind. The weather can be quite unfriendly down near KI, especially in Backstairs Passage, which is the stretch of water between the mainland and KI, just before you get there. We really got buffeted around. I almost forgot that children, who of course didn't want coffee, had to be offered cordial, usually the bright orange sort, which caused many of them to throw up, particularly if the flight was a bit rough. The fun part came when taking away sick bags with orange-coloured liquid and providing the children with damp cloths for their parents or carers to clean them up. We scored the job of cleaning the aircraft seats. We'd wipe them with Dettol and wet cloths, then request the cleaners to do a more thorough clean upon return to Adelaide. A hostess report to the chief hostess was always necessary for anything out of the ordinary, even small matters. This covered us as well as the airline.

I can't believe that I never dropped a tray or spilt hot coffee on someone. My guardian angel perhaps? I did however manage to hit a few people in the head while resting the tray on the seat tops. If the person in front leaned back too far, then that's what happened, or if some fool tried to recline their seat while the coffee service was in progress. Still, no one ever sued for concussion.

I'm sure the coffee service was very entertaining for most passengers, because it was so fraught and crazy. Incredibly, sometimes a passenger would hold up their cup for more coffee. No way; the wheels were practically on the tarmac!

These flights were immensely popular, especially on public holiday weekends. Easter, for instance, was a key time and there were always one or two rosters which involved KI marathons. Over and back four times, which meant eight coffee services; except if it was kids, which meant more sick bags to dispose of. We had to hold the sick bags discreetly behind our backs with a smile pasted onto our face. The smile wasn't obligatory, but most of us managed it. Most girls tried to go for the Good Friday roster, in which this tour of duty was over and done with early in the day. The Friday return flights never had as many passengers. Then you could enjoy your weekend and pity the poor girls doing Easter Monday afternoon, which was the reverse – the full complement of forty or forty-four flew back to Adelaide, and were rowdier and smellier and sicker than they had been flying over. People who were camping often didn't get around to showering, hence the bad smell in the cabin.

Regardless of the day or the weather, we'd be strapped into our seats for landing, hair in place, lipstick freshly applied, smiling and ready to repeat the performance on our return flight.

I'm afraid to say that in my early days, I'd more often than not tumble down the stairs to say goodbye to the passengers, with hat askew, lippy half on and minus my gloves (a real no-no), which would be frowned upon by the senior hostess if she was the picky type, and some were. I never quite managed to be Miss Perfect, but for the most part I believe I did a pretty good job and looked the part.

5

All the Pretty Aeroplane Ladies in Their Technicolor Uniforms

In 1974, management of Ansett Airlines of South Australia decided it was time for their hostesses to have new uniforms. The raspberry-coloured outfit that I'd started with had apparently been worn for a number of years. ASA had always had different attire from Ansett Mainline, even though they were part of the same company. A few years later, this was to change, but in early 1974, we began wearing dresses, coats and hats in brilliant yellow or green. Try not to screw your noses up; the effect was better than you might think and highly individual: the shades of green and yellow were clear, pretty colours, not murky or dull.

Our two check hostesses at the top of the list were allowed to choose their colour and the rest of us were allocated either green or yellow, alternately, down the list. I was a green girl.

You couldn't miss us. On the darkest of days, there we'd be, prancing in twos across the tarmac like canaries or a pair of parrots, or a canary and a parrot.

Of course the uniforms got mixed reviews. Apparently, some of the Ansett mainline girls thought our new outfits were fun and cute; others turned up their noses (well, yes, of course they were jealous). Other staff around the airport didn't forget to voice their opinions either. In another chapter, I mention how people thought it was OK to say anything they liked within our hearing, complimentary or not. I thought perhaps someone might nickname us Aeroplane Jellies, or worse, sing the jingle. However, one of our captains used to call the green girls Jolly Green Giants, which did a lot for the ego when signing on, especially if you were having a fat day. Captain Tooth would say, 'Ah, two Jolly Green Giants flying today.' At other times he called us all Aeroplane Ladies, which was preferable. I don't remember whether he had a specific nickname for the yellow girls.

Here's what comprised our new get-ups. The green girls had two or three (they needed frequent washing) dresses in plain green with short sleeves striped in yellow, brown, orange and green. We also had an overcoat in green, a green short jacket with long sleeves and a little pillbox hat with stripes around the outside (in the same tones as the sleeves) and a green crown. These sat pertly on the backs of our heads and were held firmly by a comb. The yellow ladies had the same, but in bright yellow. Their dresses had sleeves in stripes, the reverse colour order of the green ones. They also had a yellow coat, yellow jacket and a stripy hat with yellow crown. We were indeed a sight to behold.

These startling new uniforms were designed by a senior staff member and tailor-made by a dressmaker who lived in Glenelg, which is close to our West Beach Airport. Mrs Barratt was quite a character. At a fitting, if something didn't sit properly, she'd pull and tug it across and say, 'That'll be all right, luv,' or 'It'll be fine, luv.'

In the hostess lounge, we all used to joke about her saying, 'It'll be fine, luv.'

Would we be minus a sleeve? Or would the bodice be too tight? However, Mrs Barratt was very skilled at what she did and in the end they looked perfect: beautifully made, love them or hate them.

I personally liked my green uniform, one of the reasons being, during the green and yellow era, still in 1974, I had some studio photos taken by a top Adelaide photographer of the time. The outcome of my session was that the photographer was very pleased with the photos and asked me for permission to display one or two of them in his display case, which fronted onto King William Street, a main Adelaide thoroughfare. Naturally, I gave my consent and there I was, for all the world to see, framed in flattering light in a large head and shoulders shot, wearing my stripy hat and with my dark, shiny hair styled into a pageboy bob, which was highly fashionable at the time.

Needless to say, I was very proud of the photo and I was often recognised on the street or on board the aircraft and asked, 'Haven't I seen you somewhere before?' Of course that's a frequently used pick-up line too.

'Probably in the photographic display case on King William Street?'

'Ah yes, that's it. You must be very pleased. It's a lovely photo.'

Of course I was pleased; being admired by strangers and sometimes friends at any time of day was an ego boost. My fifteen minutes of fame was running overtime.

A definite downside of these uniforms was that the fabric was synthetic, so they felt sticky in our stinking hot summers and never warm enough in winter, even when wearing a coat as well.

It only recently occurred to me that for a passenger with a hangover, seeing bright green or yellow on an early-morning flight may not have been the best start to the day.

The bright green and yellow era ended in 1977, when we changed uniforms yet again; this time to conform with Ansett mainline in their orange and black outfits, topped off with the beehive hats well-known at the time. They also sat on the back of the head, but were higher and more dome-shaped and yes, they did resemble beehives.

6

Market Day in Mount Gambier

I wrote in an earlier chapter about our all-day jaunts to Mount Gambier in South Australia's south-east. Following our early-morning flights into the city, the ASA crew were always accommodated in the town's best hotels. The same group of people usually flew back with us in the late afternoon, having finished their business dealings for the day. The rest of the time was our own to do with as we wished, and sometimes the four of us would enjoy the short walk into the main shopping area, for a bite of lunch. Sometimes just the two girls went out while the pilots slept, lazy blighters.

It so happened that one of the air hostesses, Trish, a friend of mine, knew an excellent butcher in Mount Gambier. Some years before, her parents had run a motel here and purchased their meat from Mr McDowell (not his real name). One day, Trish took me into his shop. A friendly and amiable man, he remembered Trish and her family. On her recommendation, I bought a kilo of Mr McDowell's beef sausages.

'They're the best,' Trish told me.

Back in the hostess lounge in Adelaide that evening, we told some of the other hostesses about our sausage spree, plus showed any clothes or shoes we may have bought. Comparing purchases was a popular pastime after a day away. Any girls present in the hostess lounge were required to display and admire purchases, with well-timed oohs and aahs and take note of recommendations on boutiques, shops and so on.

The sausage trend caught on. Mr McDowell did great business, especially in his beef sausages, which really were the best, and most of the ASA crew were buying up.

The next discovery was that one of the trainee pilots had family with a cheese-making business in Mount Gambier. He offered to get us large two, maybe even three-kilo blocks of cheese, which we'd order and pay for through him; so that was another business going swimmingly. The cheese was some of the best I've ever had, and in later years, after finishing flying, my husband and I visited a specialty cheese shop in Mount Gambier, run by this same family. We thought it was still the tastiest cheese in South Australia.

Then someone, I've forgotten who, stumbled upon a wonderful country bakery. There were a few others in Mount Gambier, as it's a large country town, but this one was fairly new and located down a side street, off the main road. I think two of the hostesses must have had a delectable vegetable slice for lunch. The woman serving in the bakery told them that they also did extra-large ones which were great for families. Anyway, word went around like wildfire and before long many of us were ordering these super-delicious, long vegetable slices.

Does it sound like market day at the Mount Gambier airport? It was, just about, and after a short time, the various businesses used to offer to drive our goodies to the airport in time for the return flight to Adelaide. They delivered our shopping direct to the door of the Fokker Friendship. How's that for service? Sometimes the airport staff would collect the ordered food from the various shops if they were doing a run into the town. This was yet another example of how spoilt we were. Besides this, all the food was very reasonably priced and I know that sometimes a few dollars were taken off because we were flight crew.

I'd come home after an all-day jaunt with a bag full of sausages and a big block of cheese almost large and solid enough to hit someone with, besides one or two vegie slices, as sometimes I'd buy an extra one for my parents. I don't remember whether we had a freezer at that time; if we did, it was most likely only a fridge freezer, so the food was consumed quickly.

I frequently used to bid for the Mount Gambier trip, which was always a favourite, due to its having the prettiest scenery and all the interesting shops. I should mention here that we used to refer to these Mount Gambier market trips as sausage specials, which of course always included the purchase of cheese and vegie slices. I frequently had to stock up on the cheese blocks, as my husband is a keen cheese eater and a block wouldn't even last a fortnight. These days, his doctor tut-tuts if he eats too much cheese, or too much of anything really, but that's another story.

At times, we also used to purchase fish fillets or crayfish from Kangaroo Island, or Ceduna on the west coast of South Australia; so you can see, we were very well catered for.

Today, I still have a soft spot for Mount Gambier and every few years, when we're holidaying in the south-east, I love passing through or even staying for a night and there are many good places in which to stay. Two of my favourites have been Jens Hotel in the main street – a lovely old-fashioned building with iron lace on the balcony, a massive solid staircase and cosy rooms – and the Big 4 Caravan Park, in one of their cabins among beautiful tall gum trees. I recommend the Mount for a holiday, with its sometimes azure Blue Lake, sinkholes, complete with gardens which provide homes for possum families, and nearby caves. And yes, the cheese is still some of the tastiest on the market.

7

Do You Remember?

This chapter is a little bit of nostalgia from days of travel gone by. Some of you will remember of course and my, how times have changed.

The Qantas kangaroo route was introduced by Qantas in 1947 to fly to the UK and Europe via Asia and the Middle East. I wasn't around in that year, so you see, I'm not that old, but I remember the kangaroo route being advertised on telly and on radio in 1965. I certainly became familiar with it when I started flying with Airlines of South Australia and I flew to London several times via the kangaroo route, while on holiday. There was also the Southern Cross route and the fiesta route. Anyway, it's all on the net if you'd like to read it and there are some gorgeous old photos as well. You can see one of them on the opposite page which features a Constellation aircraft, introduced by Qantas to fly the kangaroo route. It was the first pressurised aircraft, which certainly made the long flight of four days more comfortable for passengers.

Do you remember traveller's cheques? What fun it was carrying a wad of them in your handbag or money belt and being careful to only sign a certain section of them upon purchase and in front of the shop assistant.

Even more fun was the crossing of different European borders and having to come to grips with an entirely new currency. There were so many different ones: French francs, Swiss francs, Belgian francs, and Italian lira. At least with the lira, you never had to worry about whether you had the right change or not. The Italians just used to give you a handful of lollies. Simple! Then came Austrian schillings,

Ansett Airlines ticket with sticker showing flight number and seat allocation.

A Constellation aircraft, used on the kangaroo route from late 1940s to late 1950s.

German marks, Dutch guilder and of course kroner from the various Scandinavian countries. Sometimes this would happen daily. For those who were mathematically challenged, like me, it was a real headache. By the time I arrived back in England, my base, I'd forgotten all about English pounds!

Suitcases without wheels. It's a wonder there isn't a whole generation of lopsided people with assorted neck, back and shoulder problems. Hauling heavy suitcases onto the European trains with their high steep steps was quite a feat and my suitcase was always heavy. In spite of being an air hostess, I've somehow never managed to travel light, much as I've tried. My suitcase was always full of different pairs of shoes, platform shoes back in the 70s, to go with my many different outfits, and assorted gifts and even more clothes as the journey progressed. I was a real clothes horse and wouldn't have been caught dead looking dowdy in Europe. What would people think of Australians?

Australians could enter New Zealand without needing a passport. There were no security checks or random checks. I remember the first random security checks being carried out in about 1974 and they always seemed to pick Melbourne or Whyalla flights. What was it about Melbourne and Whyalla? I did learn later that Whyalla especially had a mixed ethnic population, some of whom were dodgy and regarded with suspicion. That was the era of events as portrayed in *Underbelly* on the TV in recent years.

We read Arthur Frommer's famous *Europe on 5 dollars a Day*. Was that ever possible? Did we dream it? I used to love reading my copy and found some great places to stay in various cities and towns in Europe and London. Great advice, too. Later it became $10 a day and then $15. I think I stopped travelling about then and the next time I caught up with it in a bookshop it was $40 a day. Yikes! Now they have *Lonely Planet* guides which are very good too, but I'll always have a soft spot for the iconic Frommer books. Some years ago, I managed to lose my Frommer's *Europe on 5 Dollars a Day*, but happily a few months back I came across one on the bookshelf of the Sunflower Shop (the op shop where I used to volunteer). I read it sometimes and indulge in a nostalgia session. Delightful!

I experienced the Biba Boutique in Kensington High Street, London. How I wish I'd actually bought something wonderfully Bo-Ho and alternative there. My daughter would have been rapt! It's one of my great life regrets not doing so. I recently read that Anna Wintour, the current editor of *American Vogue* magazine, worked at Biba when it first opened.

The tea, coffee, and soft drink trolleys were standard on British trains. Complete with British Rail sandwiches and British Rail fruit cake. I thought it was so civilised the way they'd trundle round to your compartment and serve the drinks and snacks, along that corridor outside the carriage. Do they exist any more? These days you mostly have to trek through a series of carriages to the dining/catering car, which is usually the one furthest from where you're sitting, and freak out with the speed and rattle when going from one carriage to another. I'm talking about other countries, though. I haven't been in the UK for ages.

British European Airways or Dan Air? British European Airways was a division of British Airways and, as the name suggests, flew between London and European capitals. While looking online for references to BEA, I found a photo of the old West London Air Terminal building, from where buses used to leave for Heathrow. I had taken one of these buses on a number of occasions. It was strange looking back down the years to an empty building which had once been a bustling hive of activity. The effect was quite eerie.

Dan Air was a small airline based in Ashford, Kent, and flew over to Beauvais in France. It took about forty minutes, I think, to cross the English Channel. Dan Air may have flown other routes too, but that was my introduction to it in 1974. The day I flew was in early June, but it might as well have been winter. The weather was drizzly and misty and I couldn't see any of the Channel or France until we landed. I was trying to remember what type of aircraft I flew in. It may have been a Convair or a Viscount, but definitely one of the older planes.

8

Fond Memories of Old Airports

Everyone thinks that the era in which they lived is the best. I have tried not to say, 'In my day, travel was much easier and more fun' However, I've changed my mind, because actually I think it was, and here are the reasons why.

Aircraft seats seemed wider. Yes, I realise that I may have become a bit broader in the last thirty years; I can blame the kids for that. I'm nowhere near the extension seat belt size, though, and I can still have quite a comfortable trip; there's just not as much arm space. Planes weren't always chock-a-block full and there was frequently an empty seat or seats nearby to take advantage of.

There were no nasty little mini TV screens prised into seat backs. Instead there was a lovely big screen that the cabin crew lowered from somewhere in the ceiling, I think, onto cabin bulkheads. Of course, I'm referring to years gone by and it was usually only international flights that showed movies. Today of course, many domestic aircraft display this feature too. Is it just me, or does anyone else hate those poky screens? I'd rather sit by the window and watch cloud patterns. I must say some music is always nice, but I can do without the other. I don't mind if you think I'm old-fashioned.

Airports were smaller and easier to navigate and the entire atmosphere seemed more relaxed and less aggressive. Of course airports now have to be much bigger, but I'm just glad I was around when they were smaller, more personal.

There were no E tickets. People went to the relevant airline office in the city to buy a ticket, or from an agency if they lived in a country town.

Me, standing in the car park of the old Adelaide airport terminal. The air traffic control tower is visible in the background.

They came away with a glossy little booklet with a picture of an aircraft or an air hostess on the front. Upon checking in, a sticker displaying the flight number and seat allocation was placed on the front.

Once at the airport, for those who had some time to kill, you could wander out onto a viewing deck to watch aircraft push back and taxi out for take-off. You could get high on the smell of avgas. Yes, I really do like that smell; for me, it's very evocative, hearing the scream of the jet engines and almost being blown away by the wind that often howls around airports. Anyway, you could watch the whole procedure from beginning to end until the plane was just a tiny speck in the distance…

DC9 aircraft – along with the Boeing 727-100 the first jets to appear in Adelaide.

There's no doubt that today's airports are geared more to physical comfort, and of course much encouragement is given to people spending their money. You can shop till you drop if you wish, at book/magazine outlets, boutiques, various duty-free shops and even specialty gourmet food and wine shops. For example, at Adelaide Airport, South Australian wines feature prominently in Icons, along with the delectable Haighs chocolates. There's always an ATM placed conveniently nearby. There's any number of cafés, there's travelators, lifts, escalators and huge car parks. I mustn't forget the covered walkways that lead to your aeroplane door. They're a brilliant idea and have reduced the need for a walk across a wind-blown or rainy tarmac or the risk of being run over by a massive incoming jet.

There's lots of clever things, but I still think some of the old airport magic got lost along the way.

9

Terrorism

Before 1973 or 1974, there were often no security checks at major airports or else random ones carried out very casually. They began to be more serious about them around 1975. Of course it was becoming necessary, because the world was seeing an increase in terror attacks which targeted airliners. I recently read online that in 1969, there were forty hijacking attempts on planes in the United States. Even at that stage, most airlines were against the idea of checking passengers individually. Between 1968 and 1972, hijackers took over an airliner every other week.

Even in Australia, we had our first, and hopefully last, hijacking. November 1972 saw a very nasty incident take place in Alice Springs, in the Northern Territory, on an Ansett Airlines Fokker 27. In brief, a man boarded the plane in Adelaide with a concealed sawn-off Armalite rifle and a sheath knife strapped to his leg. Half an hour before landing in Alice Springs, he emerged from the toilet and threatened one of the hostesses with the gun. He demanded to see the captain, who informed him he couldn't speak with him as he was too busy landing the plane. The hostesses asked the man to be seated for landing and surprisingly, he complied. Once on the ground, police negotiated with him. Apparently, he wasn't demanding money, but wanted to commit suicide in a spectacular fashion by parachuting into a remote area, and survive as long as he could before shooting himself. The incident ended with an undercover policeman being shot, but fortunately not killed, and the hijacker running away, whereupon he shot himself. The whole story is online and if you Google Ansett Airlines Flight 232, you can read the story in full. It would have been terrifying for all concerned. I believe the two air hostesses handled the situation brilliantly and they both carried on flying for quite some time. I met one of them once and she was a lovely girl. I also flew on the very aircraft where the event took place. I must say I'm glad that was before I started.

Some well known terrorist groups in the 70s and 80s were the PLO, Bader-Meinhof and the IRA. Hijacking chapters were now written into our hostess manuals and discussed during emergency revalidation lectures, which happened yearly. The parts that I remember from these lectures are that we were instructed to appear to assist the hijacker within reason, and ask them to put down any weapon that they may have been holding, as it made us nervous. (Yeah, really.) Also to try to keep the hijacker drinking lots of fluid, except alcohol, so hopefully they'd need to visit the toilet. Well, like I said, early days.

At least back then, you didn't have to be concerned with how much liquid you were taking on board, or whether there was an errant nail file or small scissors hiding in the bottom of a bag.

Air travel was certainly changing, but no one could have foreseen the terrible events which have forced air travel to be as it is now, as we can see from the many news stories on the TV and online. Anything can happen to anyone at any time, so a great deal of time and money and expertise goes in to creating a safe environment.

10

Leerers and Lechers

It goes without saying that air hostesses attracted a fair amount of male attention, both wanted and unwanted. Most of us were used to blokes ogling us or hitting on us. Generally, we shrugged it off and got on with our job. After all, we were always very busy and our time was taken up with the important business of caring for all our passengers. Also, on shorter flights, it was hard to find time to talk to people, let alone give them your phone number. You had more chance of meeting someone in a high-decibel disco or club, and most people know how hard that is. I was very wary about giving my phone number and I don't remember ever doing so.

Naturally it was fun being asked out sometimes, and occasionally I was tempted. A handsome young American bloke asked me for my phone number after a Whyalla flight. He said he was on his way to Melbourne but would be back in Adelaide a few days later. I declined to give it, so he asked my co-hostess whether she knew it, but of course she sternly said that we weren't allowed to give out phone numbers (and rightly so). I, of course, thought, 'Damn, maybe I've missed out on a fun date.' However, chances are he used the same line on other flights and I'm very happy the way my life has worked out.

The other one that comes to mind was a young Russian bloke who was travelling with a music and dance troupe. He had black eyes and unruly black hair and I thought he was so gorgeous and exotic that I almost dropped his coffee when I handed it to him. Thank goodness I didn't; it would have been mortifying. I don't even remember whether he actually asked me out. I think it was a case of wishful thinking.

Amazingly, many blokes thought it was OK to comment on our appearance within our hearing. They included staff around the airport: pilots, traffic officers, now known as passenger service officers, crewing, caterers, loaders and cleaners and of course passengers. They'd point out to us whether we'd gained or lost weight, whether or not they liked a new hairdo or even if they thought we had too much make-up and so on.

Taxi drivers were some of the worst offenders. When I first joined, there were many girls who caught taxis and were issued with taxi service orders (TSOs), which meant the company paid. The drivers at the time came to know us and they were also familiar faces. In the hostess lounge, we'd compare notes on the various drivers and often we'd have a good laugh, although some of the behaviour of the drivers was far from funny.

One taxi driver used to make a habit of turning round while driving and staring pointedly at our legs for much longer than was safe, and more than one of us told him to keep his beady eyes on the road. I used to plonk my handbag over my knees. Yes, our dresses were quite short but that behaviour was inexcusable. Yet another told me he liked natural-looking girls and that he hated too much make-up. So, who cares? I'd done nothing to start a conversation with him and his remark came out of the blue. Was it a message aimed at me? If so, it made me want to apply even more make-up.

Another taxi driver developed a crush on me and asked me out to Christmas dinner. I'd been daydreaming, though certainly not about him, and when he asked me out we were pulling up outside the airport door and it was time to exit the cab, thank goodness. I rather absently and sarcastically answered, 'Oh, yeah, brilliant idea.'

He took me literally and told all the other girls from ASA how beautiful I was and that I'd agreed to go to Christmas dinner with him. I soon set them straight on that.

One morning, the taxi driver who took me to the airport told me that I looked just like Kim Novak. For those of you who are very young and only familiar with Jennifer Lawrence or Scarlett Johannson, Kim Novak was a blonde-bombshell movie star. This driver told me she was his ideal woman and that I ought to get my hair dyed blonde (I was a brunette) so I'd look just like her. Creepy. I think this bloke had stalker potential. However, I was sort of pleased that I apparently looked like Kim Novak; after all, she was a very attractive woman. I just wished it had been someone else who'd told me.

On a flight to Whyalla one afternoon, I was asked out by a middle-aged man who was a regular on our flights and who happened to be a doctor. As I was only about twenty-three or four, I thought that by mid-forties or fifties, life was just about over. Anyway, this bloke was seated in an exit row, and as I was the junior on board, I was obliged to sit next to him. He seized his opportunity and asked me out on a date, but like I said, I thought he was ancient and turned him down.

I later related this to my co-hostess and she looked at me as if I'd taken leave of my senses.

'You said no?' She seemed quite upset and was aghast. 'But he's a doctor and quite rich.'

'So what. I don't care and I'm not interested,' I told her.

Status and money were never factors which attracted or impressed me. They still don't. I can only assume, by her reaction, that she would have leapt at the chance of a date with the good doctor and considered me very strange because I didn't. Too bad for her that she was married.

Another stalker alert, though we didn't use phrases like that back then, occurred when one of the Moomba blokes declared his undying love for me. Yes, on every Moomba flight when he was travelling and on which I was working, he always let me know, and one time, even told my co-hostess that he wanted to have an affair with me. What a nerve. She told him to forget it and that I was happily married. Apparently that didn't bother him. He was married too and, as it happened, I'd seen him in the airport that morning, saying goodbye to his wife and kids. I was appalled, but luckily I never saw him again after that and in late 1984, I resigned from flying.

Another incident occurred shortly after I'd married John in 1980. I was flying down to Mount Gambier and a bloke on board asked me out while I was serving breakfast. By now, I was of course wearing my wedding ring and thought I'd be free of the random chat-ups, but no, this bloke asked me to go to the Mount Gambier races with him, which must have been on that day. I was so aghast that he'd ask out a married girl, that I was a bit lost for words and could only come out with, 'No thanks. I think it's going to rain.' How lame was that? I couldn't believe that was my answer.

Later, on landing, my co-hostess sat next to him and he told her that he ran a restaurant at one of the beachside suburbs.

He said, 'You come and you bring your friend,' meaning me.

Some blokes were incorrigible.

Life was quite a minefield, but by now you could be forgiven for thinking, 'Wow, this lady really has tickets on herself. Did she make it all up?'

I promise, it's all true, but because it's so long ago, it just seems funny and I'm having a good laugh as I write. We were an attractive bunch of girls and we all had moments like these.

My husband reminded me to include a South Australian politician of the day who will have to remain nameless. He's probably dead by now, at least I hope so, but I'd better be discreet. The MP was a regular on our flights and he always turned up late, so late in fact that the aircraft engines were both turning and the door of the Friendship was just about to be closed. The person in question would saunter over to the aircraft with a smirk on his face. The only ones allowed to be rude to him were the captains, who could and did get away with saying anything they pleased, not that it seemed to worry this bloke. Anyone else would have been terminated quick smart. Once on board, our MP took his seat and reclined it as far back as possible. He knew very well that the regulations stated seats in the upright position and so on, but he just liked the girls having to bend over him and bring his chair upright, all the while wearing his ghastly supercilious smirk. He pulled the same stunt for landing too. He was loathed and detested by all of us and we groaned when we saw him coming. He was never polite or friendly to us, even though he knew our faces well; just sleazy.

Speaking of sleaze, another unpleasant habit practised by most male members of staff, when aboard the aircraft immediately before doors closed and headcount carried out, was to hold onto our waist when passing us in the aisle. There were other things that they could have hung onto, but they just liked the excuse to put their hands on either side of our waists or hips.

I must relate one incident which we all found very funny, if also really crude. On Monday evenings, we used to bring back a group of engineers from Moomba on the gas fields which border South Australia and Queensland. This group was especially rowdy and a bit wild. They'd been away from home for two to three weeks and hadn't seen wives/girlfriends and so on. I suppose they were in holiday mode.

As we opened the aircraft doors and came down the stairs, they chorused, 'Hey girls, show us yer bits.'

Well, you know what rhymes with bits, so I won't spell it out. On board about half an hour later, they'd all fallen asleep and we were left in peace. However, the blokes who remained awake were in the habit of reading lewd, sexist magazines. When we came to serve them their drink or meal, we had to take care to avert our eyes, as sometimes these magazines had explicit, very unpleasant photos which they made no effort to conceal.

Still on the subject of Moomba flights, I was once seated next to a male passenger, who, as we were taking off, complained loudly about not knowing what he would do without a woman for three weeks. You've probably seen on movies where people, children particularly, put their hands over their ears and say 'la, la, la, la' so they can't hear what's being said? Well, I felt like doing that.

The above incident was fairly unthreatening, but there were times when it would have been good to have had the power to make harassment claims, as is the case today. The attitude of the public was that we were air hostesses. What did we expect? We were made to think that we ought to be grateful and flattered. It was also suggested that somehow we'd invited this attention. Absolutely not.

A sign of the times, I suppose, that we weren't able to take action, but no doubt today's cabin crew still experience similar incidents. I think it would have been useful to have been issued with -swats and every time someone tried something really cheeky or sleazy we could have whacked them over the head with the swat. Everyone else would have seen it and the offender could have been shamed. On the other hand, why didn't we ever consider the use of the rubber truncheon, located in the flight compartment with the pilots? That would have given them something to think about.

11

'Doing the Continental'

The next few chapters are devoted to very memorable moments of holidays I spent in Europe during the years 1974 to 1983. Thus the title 'Doing the Continental', after a song title featured in a very old 1934 movie called *The Gay Divorcee*. My, how times and word meanings have changed. It starred Fred Astaire and Ginger Rogers. I remember seeing it on telly back in the 70s sometime but I know many of you won't have seen it at all. It's glamorous, old Hollywood personified and the dancing by Fred Astaire and Ginger Rogers is breathtaking. It was a good movie, though very dated, but the song 'Doing the Continental' was fun.

In June 1974, I took off for my first England and European tour. Air hostesses usually received a generous discount of seventy-five per cent from overseas airfares; however, you had to have worked with the company for a year. I'd only been flying for eleven months, but I was so anxious to visit that part of the world that I took an under-twenty-six special fare with BOAC (now called British Airways). Of course it was all very exciting and my uncle and aunt who lived in Sydney came to Kingsford Smith airport to see me off. We drank champagne while waiting for the boarding call. In those days, Adelaide didn't have an international airport and you needed to fly to Sydney or Melbourne or Perth to connect with an international carrier.

This was also my first experience of flying in a 747. As I boarded, I was somewhat taken aback by the sheer length and width of the cabin. I can't remember where I was seated, although I had a window seat on the port side and a pretty good view. There were also two vacant seats next to me, which, as you might remember me saying in an earlier chapter, would be unlikely to happen today. It was only after a couple of stiff gin and tonics started to wear off that I suddenly realised that I didn't know anyone on board and was going to visit a completely foreign part of the world, twelve thousand miles from Australia and no one there knew me either. It was a bit scary, but I pushed down the lonely feeling and concentrated on enjoying the ride. We stopped en route at Kuala Lumpur, Bombay before it became Mumbai, Tehran (yes, really) and, after twenty-six hours of flying, landed in London. Yes, Australia to London and Europe is a real marathon, though I think today there aren't as many stops, which cuts off some of the time.

I must say that I was quite freaked out by the size of the arrivals hall at Heathrow. Nothing had quite prepared me for something as immense and busy as this place. After clearing customs, I took a double-decker red bus into the BOAC terminal.

London was a bit of a shock too. I'd been imagining a city a little bigger than Sydney, but this city didn't even come close. No, it appeared to be about ten times more massive and I must say that I was so overwhelmed I nearly turned around and caught the next flight home. I came to know the meaning of the word metropolis. Suddenly I wasn't feeling so grown-up and sophisticated any more. I'm glad I didn't go home and in time I grew to absolutely adore London, but more about that later.

I was only in London for about twenty-four hours before I caught a taxi to the Victoria coach station to meet up with my tour group. I was jet-lagged, but it was nice to have conversations with the people I was going to be travelling with for the next twelve days. The coach took us to Ashford in Kent and I remember admiring the green fields of the English countryside. From Ashford we crossed the English Channel with Dan Air to Beauvais in France and it was from there that I fell in love with Europe and made lots of new friends along the way.

I recall one of the first famous landmarks I saw was the huge Beauvais cathedral, which is the fifth-largest Gothic cathedral in the world, I believe. It's 153 metres high, or 502 feet. It dominates the scene around the whole town.

We began in France, in a gorgeous little town called Beaune, then Nice on the Riviera, Italy (taking in Florence, Rome and Venice), Innsbruck, Switzerland, then Luxembourg, the Black Forest in Germany and finally Paris. This is just a general description and I'll fill in some details later.

I was ecstatic to be in Europe and just loved it. Of course, being June it was early summer and the weather was fine and warm, most of the time. The flowers were out everywhere and I was delighted to see fields full of colourful wild flowers along the way. I wondered at all the really old, sometimes ancient buildings, the cobbled streets and the stylish way the people dressed and wore their clothes. Later, when I returned home, I went out and purchased European fashion magazines and found a good dressmaker who could draft patterns by looking at the pictures. I enjoyed having something very individual to wear that also reminded me of Europe.

The food too; how could I forget the food and the wine? I had a Kir Royale cocktail for the very first time, pastries and delectable chocolates. I even learnt to enjoy European beer, which is something that I never expected to like. I'm rather ashamed to admit to looking down my nose at women who drank beer on my flights. I considered them rough, as did many of my co-hostesses. What a silly bunch of snobs we were.

Before I continue, I thought that I should describe the Kir Royale to you: it's a French cocktail, created by a priest, Canon Felix Kir. He was a hero in the French Resistance during World War Two, besides which he was once a mayor of Dijon. The wonderful cocktail Kir consists of crème de cassis, and is topped with white wine. For the Kir Royale, the cassis is topped with champagne or sparkling wine instead. That's the one I drank. Go, Felix. Have I made you want one? Me too, as I haven't had one since that evening in 1974. Actually, I think I may have had two or more, but who's counting?

I had so much fun in Europe that I thought I'd died and gone to heaven and had to keep pinching myself to really believe I was there. I hope you enjoy the next few chapters, which describe some fun events and some not-so-fun, when things didn't quite work out as expected.

12

Grasse Romeo

Europe was, and I'm sure still is, full of would-be Romeos. I was continually being offered dinner, private tours of whatever city we happened to be in, free drinks (not to be consumed under any circumstances) and once, even an invitation to visit one German Romeo's boat. Even at twenty-three, I hadn't come down in the last shower, and a year's air hostessing had been a real education. A firm 'no' and these blokes were onto the next girl, undeterred by my refusal.

The best Romeo I encountered was in the town of Grasse, known as the perfume capital of the world. Probably many of you have been there. Grasse is perched high in the Alpes Maritimes, above the French Riviera. It's a beautiful part of the world and on the day I visited, a balmy summer's day in early June 1974, the gardens were at their most colourful and smelling their sweetest. Enticing scents of roses, tuber roses, orange blossom and rose geranium mingled in the warm Riviera air.

Stepping inside to the fragrance factory and shop was somewhat overwhelming, as there were so many things from which to choose. As was usual in my twenties, I really used to splash the cash and this time was no exception. I took my many purchases to the cashier, who happened to be a young, very good-looking, flirty French bloke. I was single, with no obvious boyfriend or husband hovering around, and so I was lavished with plenty of attention, which suited me nicely at that stage of my life.

I should mention here that I was pretty clueless in working out all the different currencies in relation to the Australian dollar. I mentioned the challenge of different currencies earlier, and I'm pretty sure I lost quite a bit of money in conversions, which I couldn't really be bothered to work out anyway. I knew I had plenty of money with me and so I decided I wasn't going to let finances bother me at least until I returned to Australia. I was just out to have fun and spend as much as possible.

Flirty cashier man joked, teased and pretended to confiscate my passport. After I'd made my payment for my goodies, he put together a bag of freebies, handed them to me and said, 'These are just for you. Bonjour.'

Then it was time to say goodbye or *au revoir*. Back outside in the warm French sunshine, I inspected my surprises. There were mini lipsticks, hand creams and small bottles of perfume. One in particular I loved. It was called Mademoiselle Fragonard. I used it often and always felt pretty when I wore it, as it was youthful, fresh and floral. Although I also recall buying a variety pack of six fragrances in small gold bottles, there were none I loved as much as Mademoiselle Fragonard. Back in Australia, although I enquired many times, I never had any success in finding it. However, I think that made it all the more special, owning something unique and exclusive from the other side of the world.

Back on the Cosmos bus, my new-found friends from Canada, the UK and Queensland and I compared purchases.

I blurted out, 'What freebies did you get?'

'Freebies?' they asked. 'We didn't get any of those. Did you?'

I held up my bag and felt a bit guilty when I saw their envious expressions. However, I did not have the slightest inclination to share.

As the bus wound its way down the steep slopes, overlooking the sparkling Mediterranean, I inspected my new acquisitions with childish delight and thought of my flirty chat with Mr French Cashier. I had a feeling that I was really going to enjoy being in Europe.

(Recently, I went online and discovered that the Mademoiselle Fragonard fragrance is still available, and, like most items today, can be purchased with ease and speed. The instant gratification factor is all very nice; however, I think that I valued my little bottle all the more, because it is a distant memory of another time, when the world was a different place and I was having the time of my life on the Continent. To this day, I still keep my empty little bottle of Mademoiselle Fragonard on my dressing table for old time's sake.)

13

Waterloo

My friends and family all know I'm a huge Abba fan. Their music has enchanted me for years. I attended their Adelaide concert in March 1977. I've also seen *Mamma Mia* both on stage and screen. Actually, I saw the movie twice, and I nearly forgot that there was another movie made back in the late 70s called *Abba, The Movie*, which was put together during the time of their Australian tour. I never stopped liking them, even when at one time it became uncool to like Abba. Where did it all start?

The story has its roots in an Austrian hotel, where my Cosmos tour stayed the night. This hotel was somewhere near Innsbruck and, for some reason that I can't remember, was changed at the last minute from where we were originally supposed to stay that evening.

After dinner, as usual, I and some of the other young people on the tour went for drinks in the hotel bar. To my delight, I discovered they had a jukebox and a dance floor. I just loved to dance and it was a great way to let off steam after a long day of touring on the bus. 'Waterloo' was playing and got me in straight away. I absolutely sprang up to dance, after which I remember asking someone, 'What is that fantastic song? I love it.'

'Waterloo', they told me. 'It was the winning song at this year's (1974) Eurovision song contest. A Swedish group called Abba sang it. They're all set to be the next big thing in music.'

I'd never heard of Eurovision as, don't forget, although the world was shrinking with jet travel and TV, there was no social media and no instant way to connect with the music world as there is now.

I bounced back to the dance floor and fed the jukebox Austrian schillings all night, well, until after midnight, just so I could hear 'Waterloo' over and over again. You'll be glad to know that sometimes I stepped aside so other people could play their song of choice, but nothing did it for me like 'Waterloo'.

Funnily enough, I don't remember dancing with anyone in particular, although I probably did. Honestly, I think I'd have been just as happy to prance about by myself, although some of my new friends from the tour also danced, so it was lovely to have their company.

I think I finally tired myself out by about one a.m. and went to bed. I'm sure everyone else in the bar was quite relieved and said to each other, 'Thank God she's gone. No more "Waterloo".'

Back home in Australia, I immediately went to one of our department stores and purchased a vinyl LP called *Waterloo*. The four members of Abba were shown on the cover and I fell in love with all of them. I was so excited to hear some of their other songs. Then I went home and drove Mum and Dad crazy.

A final piece of trivia: Abba chose to fly with Ansett Airlines.

14

Green Eggs and Tehran

We've all heard of Dr Seuss's *Green Eggs and Ham*, but most of you won't know about Green Eggs and Tehran. In June 1974, on a BOAC jumbo jet, I was on the way to London for my first major trip to the UK and Europe. We landed at Tehran Airport at about five o'clock on a fine summer morning. We weren't allowed to disembark there, but took on new fuel and catering. I'll always remember stretching my stiff legs and gazing out of the door of the 747, watching a pink sunrise light up the golden minarets of a mosque. Behind the mosque, I could see a snow-capped mountain. That image has stayed with me and whenever I hear about Tehran in the news these days, I can still see that vivid image in my head. I'm quite sure that Iran would not be an easy country in which to live, but I'm glad I had that brief glimpse of what, to me, was a mysterious and exotic place.

Anyway, after take-off, breakfast was served. I removed the foil lid from the hot dish and looking at me were bacon, tomatoes, a few mushrooms – fine so far – and two green poached eggs. No, I'm not kidding. I am the kind of person who usually eats everything in sight on an airline tray, because:

a) I'm a guts
b) I have a cast-iron stomach
c) I love eating at thirty thousand feet.

However, even I was hesitant about those green poached eggs. I pressed the hostess call button, which I was loath to do, because I knew what it was like to be summoned by that insistent little ping, which didn't stop until you'd dealt with the issue. I'd been flying for

London-Bahrain

London/Frankfurt
1 hour 30 mins.

Refreshment

Frankfurt/Bahrain
5 hours 35 mins.

Dinner

Dinner

Hors d'oeuvre Salad

Saute of Beef Bourguignonne
Vegetables in Season

Baked Apple — Rum Sauce

Cheese

Coffee

Carafes of Red or White Wine available
Au. 50 cents each

Bahrain-Bangkok

6 hours 25 mins.

Breakfast

Breakfast

Fruit Compote

Tomato Omelette
Grilled Bacon

Bread Roll   French Biscotte

Marmalade

Coffee   Tea   Chocolate

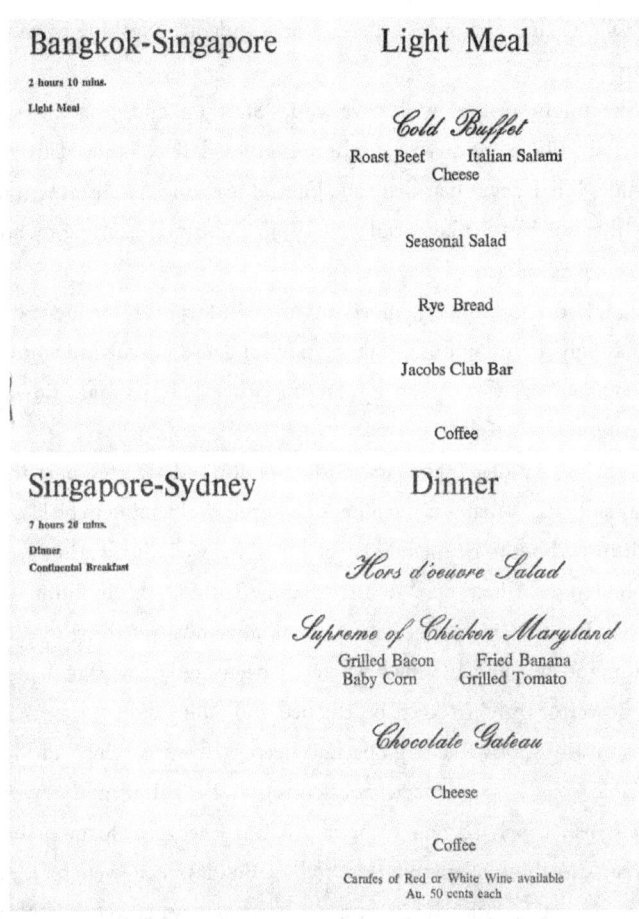

1976 Qantas menu given to passengers.

nearly a year by then with ASA and people used to press their call button for the most inane reasons. For example, young blokes often pressed the call button in order to request yet another beer, even when it was blatantly obvious that we were just about to land. Of course, the answer was a firm no. People also wanted to ask whether they could make a last-minute trip to the toilet. Again, no, for the same reason. Anyway, back to my story. The BOAC hostess duly came and, as I suspected she might be, was a bit annoyed and grumpy. I at least managed to be polite when called.

'Oh, it's only the ovens,' she said off-handedly. 'Nothing to worry about.'

She might just as well have said, 'Shut up and just eat your breakfast,' like a mother to a whining child. I felt chastised by her attitude, but I nevertheless ate the lot and was fine. I'll also mention here that we had actual metal cutlery. Just another example of how things have changed.

I flew on to London, glued to my window seat for a view of increasingly mountainous terrain by now, and also watched the movie, which was *Forty Carats* starring, among others, Liv Ullman, Edward Albert and Gene Kelly.

I anxiously waited for our arrival into London and had a few butterflies in my stomach. What was the other side of the world going to be like?

It turned out to be the holiday of a lifetime; well, the first in a series of holidays of a lifetime. We arrived quite early in the morning and nobody had told me about jet lag. Later, after finally settling into the Kensington bed and breakfast where I'd been booked to stay, I made the fatal error of lying down on the bed and falling asleep. I awoke at one a.m. and wasn't able to go back to sleep, as I was starving. All I had available to eat were a few cracker biscuits from the airline meal tray, and a Mars bar, which I'd bought because I was jet-lagged, foggy-brained and couldn't think of anything else to buy. Besides, there were no tea or coffee-making facilities in my room, so I had only water to drink. None of these things kept the hunger pangs at bay, and I had to wait until I was at Victoria coach station about eight that morning to buy some decent food. The story continues in the chapter 'Doing the Continental'.

The journey back home to Australia was equally tiring, especially after a month of partying and burning the candle at both ends. Even twenty-three-year-olds succumb to fatigue. On my return to Adelaide, having only had a few catnaps on the aircraft, I slept for eighteen hours straight, the longest I've ever slept in one hit. My mother woke me up, as I think she thought I'd lapsed into a coma from some awful disease I'd caught overseas, or maybe had even died.

15

No Room in Geneva

In February of 1978, I took my first Eurail trip through Germany, Switzerland and Austria. My American friend from Kansas City, Zelma, who I called Zee, met me in Frankfurt and we toured together. We'd met on a 1976 tour of Scandinavia and northern Germany and the following year I'd gone to the USA and visited her. We started planning our Eurail trip in a restaurant in Kansas City. I thought I was very international in those days, almost a jet-setter, except I wasn't nearly as wealthy as a real jet-setter. It sure was fun pretending, though.

In 1978, I arrived first in the morning and found us a room in the Frankfurt Airport Sheraton. By now I was entitled to all the lovely concessions that the airline offered, which included sometimes fifteen per cent off the room rate of top-class hotels. Zee flew in later to Luxembourg with Icelandic Airlines, via Chicago; then she took a train to Frankfurt and phoned me at the Sheraton. Everything ran as planned, which was a huge relief, as there'd been snowstorms in Chicago and it was quite common for American airports to close or cancel flights in the winter.

The room in the Sheraton reminded me a little of a room I'd occupied a few years previously at the Tullamarine Travelodge. It had big windows that must have lined up with one of the runways, as I was treated to a constant parade of incoming international aircraft. I just adore plane watching and not only that but there was snow falling too, so I thought it was quite magical.

Anyway, the whole trip ran like clockwork. We visited Heidelberg, Rothenburg, Munich, Salzburg and Vienna. The last stop was to be

Snowbound chalets along train route to Geneva.

Geneva and, after staying a few days, Zee would fly back to the US with Icelandic and I would fly to London with Swissair to stay with friends before heading off home to Australia with Lufthansa.

Throughout our holiday, we used the Frommer *Europe on Ten or Fifteen Dollars a Day*; prices had risen a little, but it was still excellent value. Being winter, there was never a problem getting a room for a night or two in the hotel or *pensione* of our choice. We had an absolute ball, with many coffee and cake afternoon or morning teas, an evening ballet performance of the *Nutcracker Suite* in the Vienna State Opera House, followed by hot chocolate and more cake at Vienna's Café Mozart. We danced the evening away in discos and enjoyed wonderful snowy scenery from the comfort of the European trains. I mustn't forget the shopping opportunities. Zee was very level-headed and thrifty. I, on the other hand, spent like there was no tomorrow. Had the Little Miss books been around then, I could have been *Little Miss Extravagance*.

However, on our last stop, things didn't go quite so smoothly. The train was a bit late bringing us into Geneva and we arrived at about seven in the evening, but of course being winter it was dark and cold, making it seem more like nine p.m. We jumped into the first available cab and gave the address of the accommodation we'd chosen. It was in the city centre and, as we'd so far had no problems, we thought this would be a breeze. Soon we'd be able to shower, change, find some dinner and relax for the evening.

We rang a doorbell and were greeted by a young woman who handed us a key and told us that the apartment was on the other side of the road, down a side street. We thought that was a bit weird, but duly walked over to the side street as directed and looked and looked. Try as we might, we couldn't find the relevant doorway to let ourselves in.

'Let's take the key back and try the next place in Frommer's book,' I suggested.

The area seemed deserted and felt a bit creepy.

So that's what we did. Returned the key to the girl, who shrugged in a typically French sort of way that indicated she couldn't care less. Then we jumped into another taxi and directed the driver to the address of a *pensione* which seemed to be a little further out of Geneva. He drove up and down some hills until we finally we reached the supposed *pensione*. Again, there seemed to be no one else around and a sign outside indicated that our *pensione* had turned into an aged-care home. Doesn't it make you think of that song 'Oh, What a Night'?

I was beginning to hate Geneva and I was so fed up and tired and grumpy that I was about to order the driver to take us to the most expensive hotel in the city and hang the cost. I, well we, just wanted a really nice comfy room for the last few days of our journey.

Before I could say anything, the cab driver cut in and said, 'I know a good hotel for you ladies and I'll take you there.'

'OK,' we replied wearily.

At least at this next hotel there would be signs of life. The two other locations might just as well have been on the moon. Also, by now our stomachs were growling and almost eating themselves, we were so hungry.

When we arrived, there was indeed life. The hotel suggested by the driver seemed to be full of men from all corners of the world. There wasn't a woman in sight. The taxi driver even came into the foyer with us and started chatting to the guy behind the reception desk. They obviously knew one another. Zee and I were beginning to feel uneasy and when we were shown to a room and it had no lock on the door, that did it. I was furious and felt that we were being set up, which was probably the case.

I stormed out of the room and said to Zee, 'We're not staying here, no way. It's time for plan B.'

Before leaving Australia, my cousin had given me the address and phone number of her brother-in-law and his wife, who lived in Geneva. He worked for the UN. I phoned Brian, although I felt bad having to ring someone I'd never met at nine-thirty at night. I really just wanted his advice on a pleasant and safe hotel, but he and his wife, Eva, insisted we come to their home and they would put us up.

I turned to the taxi driver, who was still in the foyer, shoved the address at him and said imperiously, 'You can take us here – this address.' I couldn't be bothered to say please. This was an order.

We sailed out of the hotel and into the night, leaving the sleazy men behind, and hopped into the cab for the last time. I noted with smug satisfaction the driver's surprise at having to drive us to a private address in what was obviously an upmarket part of Geneva.

To cut a long story short, Brian and Eva were lovely to us. They gave us food and provided a sofa-bed for us to sleep in. It must have been midnight when we tumbled into bed, falling asleep immediately.

Next day, Brian had to fly off to Dar-es-Salaam in Africa on business, and Eva visited her dentist. She was having a lot of pain from a tooth and suspected there was an abscess. This also made me feel doubly bad about barging in on them, though they never once made us feel like that.

Zee and I then had the chance to explore Geneva by daylight. The city was of course beautiful, with its lake and surrounding mountains, but had an air of crisp Swiss formality, which I was never quite able to warm to. We enjoyed our last few days together. Once, when walking along the street, I thought I recognised a well known, beautiful, black

American model who was often featured in American and international fashion magazines.

Eva was good company and her toothache was gone. It was sad when we took Zee to Geneva railway station to say goodbye. Then I made my way to Geneva airport for my Swissair flight to London. I had a brief glimpse of Mount Blanc as the plane climbed steeply through grey clouds and into clear blue sky, above the weather.

This was a truly remarkable holiday, full of wonderful youthful memories. I'm still in touch with Zee to this day. She's now married and still lives in Kansas City. In fact, I'm going to email her a copy of this travel story, which is our story.

16

Herr Pfaffenbichler

I have so many wonderful memories of people and places from my travelling days, but if I'm not careful, I'll finish up with a tome, rather than a fun, light-hearted book. Having said that, I think this particular person deserves a paragraph or two of his own, simply because he was a really likeable, if eccentric, character.

His name was Herr Pfaffenbichler (pronounced Pfaff-en-beechler) and he ran a *pensione* in Salzburg, on the snowy banks of the Salzach River. His *pensione* was called Pensione Mayburgerkai and we found him in Frommer's *Europe on Ten to Fifteen Dollars a Day.*

I was with Zee. It was 1978 and we were doing our Eurail-pass journey through Germany, Switzerland and Austria. We'd just spent a night with a lovely woman in Innsbruck and were reluctant to move on, but we were both on limited time schedules, Zee even more than me. From Innsbruck we waited for the train to Salzburg and waited and waited. I've probably mentioned that it was wintertime and I truly thought I was going to get frostbite, my feet were so cold. It was agony, so I sighed with relief when the train finally pulled in and we hopped into a cosy first-class compartment. Eurail enabled us to travel first-class and we always took advantage of that. By the way, it's very unusual for German/Austrian trains to be late, but luckily it didn't happen often.

After warming up with a hot coffee and pastry – thank goodness for the comforting powers of coffee and pastries – we scanned Frommer's guide to Salzburg and underlined in biro about three choices of *pensione*. Of course, being winter, it was much easier to get our first

Salzburg skyline, winter 1981.

In Salzburg, overlooking the Austrian Alps.

choice and this happened almost every time until we hit Geneva, as I told you in the previous chapter.

These days, you just get out your phone and dial ahead, which was something unimaginable back then. In 1978, there were no such things as mobile phones, so you had to wait until you reached your destination to phone through.

We called from a public phone in Salzburg railway station. I loved European railway stations; to me they were almost as exciting as international airports, with their hustle and bustle and trains leaving for exotic destinations. The German/Austrian/Swiss stations were always clean and efficient too.

Anyway, we rang Herr Pfaffenbichler; or rather, I rang, as I spoke a little German, so it made sense for me to do the talking.

He said, 'You come, you come right now. I have plenty rooms. You come.' I think he even apologised for not being able to come and collect us himself.

'We're on our way,' we replied.

Upon arrival, we rang the bell and turned to survey the view. The *pensione*, as I've said, was on the banks of the Salzach River and turned out to be very close to the beautiful old town of Salzburg, within walking distance. There were only houses on Herr Pfaffenbichler's side of the road, as a short distance away was the cold, grey-looking river. There was plenty of snow on the ground too.

Herr Pfaffenbichler answered the door. He was quite elderly, a bit stooped and he wore a sort of dust jacket, which I think may have been white, so he looked more like a doctor. 'Come in, come in,' he said. 'I show you your room.'

He had a habit of saying things twice, but he moved quite quickly for an older man. The room he showed us was large, had two cosy beds with fluffy continental quilts and looked out across the road, to the river. We told him we were happy with the room, agreed on the price and then we didn't see much of him until the next morning.

Zee and I were in the process of getting dressed and discussing plans for the day, when there was a knock at the door, but before we could call, 'Come in', in came Herr Pfaffenbichler with our included continental breakfast. Zee and I both had to quickly dive under the quilts again, as we were not quite respectable to answer the door.

This didn't seem to bother the old chap, who said, *'Guten morgen, Guten morgen,'* and shuffled out again.

When he'd gone, Zee and I looked at each other and burst out laughing.

The next morning, we were more prepared and ensured we'd dressed fully before the knock. Herr Pfaffenbichler didn't ever wait for the 'come in' signal, he just came. Breakfast, by the way, was delicious and consisted of fresh kaiser rolls, apricot jam (my favourite) and lots of coffee. Bliss. I can never have kaiser rolls today without thinking of Herr Pfaffenbichler and Salzburg.

We had a wonderful time in Salzburg and just loved it. I especially liked the huge glasses of wine the staff in restaurants gave you when you ordered a meal. They were almost the size of brandy balloons and helped to warm us up when we were freezing cold. We walked a lot, but one of the highlights was our *Sound of Music* tour, which took in all the locations used in the movie. I have a photo of me standing in the snow outside the summerhouse where Liesl leapt around the benches singing, 'I am Sixteen Going on Seventeen'. At the time I was twenty-six going on twenty-seven, but I didn't go leaping around on the seats. I used to slip a fair bit, not being used to the snow and ice. Besides, twenty-six going on twenty-seven doesn't have quite the same ring. We also went into the church used for the wedding scene. It was beautiful, but a bit dark and extremely ornate.

The day we left, I'll always remember Herr Pfaffenbichler came out to see us off and said to me, as he knew I was Australian, 'Australia very good country…is no boom boom.'

He's right about Australia being a good country, but I'm afraid these days, we have just as much chance of boom boom as anywhere else; well, perhaps a bit less.

I should explain here that Herr Pfaffenbichler meant bombs when he talked about boom boom. At the time, groups like the IRA and the Bader-Meinhof gang frequently used bombs in England and Europe.

Back then, a continual fear came from being overrun by communism, which was a very real concern for many of the young people we spoke to as well. Of course this was about eleven years before the wall dividing East and Western Europe came tumbling down. That was a wonderful historical event, but in 1978, no one could have imagined that ever happening.

Herr Pfaffenbichler also said, 'One day you come back and you bring your husbands.'

Well, I actually did, because in early 1981, when John and I were doing our honeymoon Eurail tour, I made sure that we stayed at Pensione Maiburgerkai again. It was as if I'd never been away. There was still plenty of snow, and Herr Pfaffenbichler was still in charge. We spent two nights with him and I think he may even have remembered me. I did jog his memory a bit by reminding him that he had told Zee and me to return and bring our husbands.

Before I end this story, I must tell you about the evening John had walked into the town by himself to buy some dinner. In Europe, sometimes we'd go to a nearby hotel for an evening meal, but at other times we'd buy food to eat in our room and enjoy a room picnic. They were always fun and we'd talk about the day's events and take a look at items we'd purchased. Anyway, this time John returned with bratwurst, which of course needs cooking. My husband was very pleased with his kilo of bratwurst. He'd even managed to ask for it in German, as I'd taught him a few basic words and he was very proud of that too.

'What are you going to do with that?' I asked him. Naturally we had no facilities for preparing a hot meal.

'Eat it of course. It's for dinner.'

'Well, we'll need a stove, because it needs cooking.' I answered.

Poor John looked aghast. He'd thought it was a cold, cooked sausage that we could eat with mustard and rolls which we had bought earlier at a bakery.

We ended up giving Herr Pfaffenbichler a present of a kilo of bratwurst, and we went for a cold snowy walk to the nearest hotel for tea, warmed up on arrival by a hearty Austrian meal and one of those fabulously huge glasses of wine.

Sadly, Herr Pfaffenbichler is probably no longer on this earth, but somehow I like to think he knows I'm writing this story about him. We had a great time, Herr Pfaffenbichler. You're a really good bloke.

17

First Class All the Way

Before I started this story, I almost changed the title to 'Live It Up', which was a popular song released in 1985 by Australian rock band Mental As Anything. It really sums up not only this chapter but the general way we were able to live back then: double income, no kids. I'm sure you get the picture. I hasten to add that we no longer indulge in this lifestyle, but it was fun for a while and we had our fling. Anyway, listen to 'Live it Up' sometime. It's a really good song.

January 1981 found John and me setting off for our honeymoon to Europe and England. We'd had a temporary honeymoon in Perth immediately after our October 1980 wedding, but this was the real one and it was to be a beauty. We each had a twenty-one-day Eurail pass for Germany, Switzerland and Austria and I think about five days planned in England. I've mentioned before that being in the airline industry definitely had its upside, with heavily discounted fares on flights and international hotels, but the downside involved lots of nerve-racking waiting, frequently until the last minute, to see if you were on or off. Still, that was part of the deal and we all accepted it.

So there we were at Tullamarine Airport in Melbourne at ten a.m., fresh, excited and dressed in our going-away outfits, as it was wise to dress well when travelling on concessional fares. The Lufthansa flight to Frankfurt wasn't due to leave until seven that evening, but the pleasant check-in staff assured us that the flight wasn't full, so they felt sure we'd be fine.

In Tullamarine there was plenty to keep a couple of airport geeks like us amused. Even back in 1981, it was a very busy airport with

Outside Frankfurt Airport, a maze of roads leading to the autobahn.

Outside the Frankfurt Airport Sheraton, the morning after arrival.

lots of incoming and outgoing flights. There were airlines we never ever saw in Adelaide and we revelled in the buzz of the international atmosphere. The weather was perfect as I recall, a gorgeous Australian summer day in the mid-twenties, so not too hot, and we spent plenty of time on the observation deck, getting high on the smell of avgas, which we both liked, being deafened by the roar of jet engines and watching foreign air traffic. Remember observation decks? John and I used to love them. Now, although we still enjoy visiting airports, you might just as well be locked in a soundproof glasshouse. Even a window seat in one of the coffee shops isn't the same any more as you can't hear the engines revving up, which adds to the buzz and general atmosphere. Just one legacy of 9/11.

Anyway, time passed and after many hours of plane-watching, we lunched in the upmarket restaurant overlooking the tarmac. As I recall, we were given a voucher to use for our meal because we had a long wait. Airlines back then were much more generous than today and so, after a good meal and several champagnes later, we went back to the Lufthansa desk for a progress report. There had been a hitch. An incoming aircraft had, upon taxiing, clipped the wing of a Malaysian plane. The Malaysian aircraft was therefore rendered US – meaning unserviceable, but in the airlines we had another name for it, which you can probably guess. To cut a long story short, this meant that our plane, the Lufthansa, now had to accommodate the extra Malaysian passengers, as both Lufthansa and Malaysian were calling in at Kuala Lumpur (also both were 747s). Departure was now to be delayed for a further two hours. Our hearts sank, but not for long. The happy outcome of this little drama was that Lufthansa let us board and upgraded us to first class. Actually, I must confess it was business class, but to us it felt like first. Besides, you should never let facts get in the way of an impressive story. An upgrade of any sort on international routes was an event so rare that it almost deserves to be recorded in the airline history books, especially as we were concessional travellers. I'm sure it helped that we had dressed in our best.

Needless to say, we swanned off to Frankfurt in blissful comfort. We were given free drinks and a choice of meals, had plenty of legroom and were attended by efficient, friendly and attractive young German people with gorgeous accents. We couldn't quite believe our good fortune. I think we half expected to be tossed out at each of our two ports of call, Kuala Lumpur and Karachi (heaven forbid), but that didn't happen. In KL, we were allowed off the plane and had time to do a little shopping. I bought a long silver necklace and two Malaysian dolls, all of which I still have. Of course by now it was night, and all the aircraft on the tarmac seemed to loom larger than by day, and the heat and humidity almost swallowed us up. We reached Karachi by early morning and there we weren't allowed to disembark, not that we minded. Karachi airport looked bleak and uninviting through heat haze and dust. Stony-faced guards with machine guns stood on the tarmac. We sank down into our cosy first-class seats and watched. Even in the 1980s there was terrorist activity. Remember the Bader-Meinhoff gang and the PLO? Political instability seemed ever present in this region.

Hours later, we landed in Frankfurt-Main, where the landscape was grey, white and snowy. We'd arrived to the enchantment of falling snow. John was absolutely mesmerised. I had been in Europe in winter before, but later in our room at the Frankfurt Airport Sheraton, he couldn't be dragged away from the window. As we were both badly jet-lagged, I thought John might actually fall asleep standing up while gazing at the snowy landscape outside.

What a start to our honeymoon. Was it all as perfect as that? Pretty close, but a few less-than-perfect events happened, a couple of which I'll tell you about later.

18

The Case of the Lost Coats in the Sacks of Potatoes

After John and I had partially recovered from our jet lag by overnighting in the lovely Frankfurt Airport Sheraton, we both agreed it was certainly an ideal place to assist in the recovery of a twenty-four-hour flight. Today they may have been able to shave a couple of hours off the time, but it still remains, I think, one of the world's longest air routes.

I somehow managed to prise John away from the snow in Germany for our flight to England. We'd allowed about five or six days based in London, which of course, in that amazing city, is never enough, but we had to allow time for our two-week Eurail trip through Germany, Switzerland and Austria. Our accommodation was in a bed and breakfast called the Vicarage, and it was in a quiet and pretty cul-de-sac off Kensington Church Street. The Kensington area is one of our favourite parts of London and we've stayed there several times.

I was pleased to be able to recommend some sightseeing, as by now I'd been to London several times. John loved London. I was quite relieved, because he hadn't been that impressed on our drive in from the airport. That was the jet lag talking, I suspect. Anyway, we had a ball and fitted so much in. We visited the Tower of London, where the guide did a particularly gruesome version of the executions that took place. We had lunch in Liberty's, followed by some fabric shopping, choosing from their myriad of colourful fabrics. Then more shopping, as you do, in Marks and Spencers and the Scotch House: evensong in St Paul's Cathedral; and even a couple of side trips to Cambridge and

Snowplough clearing snow outside our Pensione Paula in Innsbruck. The year 1981 saw the heaviest snowfall in the Alps for ten years.

Canterbury, which is almost obligatory for Anglicans. We wouldn't have missed it for the world, though. One of John's purchases in London was a Dunn and Co. Harris tweed jacket, which is something he'd always wanted. We put it into a black plastic suit pack along with another light brown suede jacket, which was a favourite of John's and mine as well, as he'd worn it on one of our early dates.

Then it was time to head back to Germany. Our first port of call was to be Heidelberg and we took the train there from the Frankfurt airport. Once again we found accommodation from the Frommer guidebook and of course being winter we never had any trouble in securing a lovely, warm, cosy room in which to make our home for a day or two. I'd been to Heidelberg before with my American friend Zee and now here I was, almost three years later, a newly-wed and showing some of what I remembered to John. He revelled in Europe and of course the snow provided a never-ending source of delight.

The next place we decided to visit was Freiburg, and it was while packing our things that morning before heading out to the station that we realised we were missing the plastic suit pack. To this day I don't know why it took us so long to realise it was missing, but it did.

The Frankfurt city skyline.

Jet lag is always a convenient excuse. After we'd paid up, we told our host about the lost coats. He was sympathetic and suggested we travel back to Frankfurt to enquire at the lost property office. We did so and the staff in Frankfurt searched but came up with nothing. They did tell us, however, that the train we'd taken would have continued to Stuttgart. The trip was only twenty minutes, they told us, and thought it was worth a try. But we had no luck in Stuttgart either. By now we had sadly accepted that the coats were gone for good and that some lucky person had found them and thought all their Christmases and birthdays had come at once. We decided that we still had two weeks of holiday to go and to write off losing the coats as a bad experience. Resolutely, we took a deep breath and plunged into the rest of our wonderful trip.

After that, things looked better, with the exception of our stay in Freiburg. Because of the rigmarole of searching in lost property offices for the coats, we were late arriving into Freiburg. We selected a hotel that had been given the thumbs up by a reader, so we went there, only to find the host in her nightgown and fairly reluctant to put us up. In the end she agreed, but explained that she couldn't (or wouldn't) provide breakfast, but we didn't care. The whole place felt unfriendly, including her massive German shepherd dog. This *pensione* was also close to the Freiburg jail, with its high walls topped with barbed wire. Creepy.

After Freiburg, we stayed in Zurich, Salzburg and Innsbruck. Salzburg was in the middle of its Mozartwoche (Mozart Week) Festival. John and I feasted on musical concerts and a ballet, and also on delicious Austrian winter comfort food, like schnitzels and strudels. There was a hitch with our luggage in Innsbruck, which was the fault of the railways, not us. We got it back later in the evening, but although it was snowing heavily, they still expected us to go to Innsbruck station to pick it up, even after we'd settled into our *pensione*, a gorgeous chalet overlooking the town. Europe was having its heaviest snowfalls in ten years. More than once, we fell into knee-deep snow.

On our route to Innsbruck through the Alps, the train had to stop frequently to enable snow from avalanches to be shovelled from off the tracks. However, we didn't care how long it took, as we were indulging in a silver-service luncheon in the dining car, while watching intricate snowflakes settle on the outside of the windows, lit by the candles on our table. That train trip is especially memorable.

Finally we came back to Frankfurt, where we had about two days left. We stayed in a hotel near the railway station, so as to be close by for our short trip back to Frankfurt-Main airport. This hotel was like something out of a movie. Indeed one of the staff reminded us of a character from *Cabaret*. The atmosphere was rather surreal and felt a bit seedy and decadent. Anyway, it was there that we decided to make one last effort to find John's missing coats, so the night before we were due to leave we presented ourselves at the Frankfurt Railway Police Station, which was an interesting experience. There were wanted posters on the wall for members of the Bader-Meinhof gang, but the police were surprisingly obliging and friendly, although it didn't seem to us as if they would be. They were both very tall and well-built, had big, heavy boots to the knee and barked orders at others. Indeed, I wouldn't have liked to be on their wrong side, but they were very kind to us. To cut a long story short, they did retrieve the coats and you won't in a million years guess where they were. Actually you might, because it's in the title of this story. They found them by grabbing hold of a poor old bloke working in one of the back offices. He looked rather nonplussed and intimidated.

The policemen, I'm afraid, shouted orders at him to hurry up. '*Schnell, schnell!*' they demanded.

They both followed the old chap to where he was working, and there lay John's coats amid sacks of potatoes. The policeman spoke to me in German and I'll swear that's what he said. My mastery of the German language was better in those days. Neither one of us had any idea how the coats could have ended up among sacks of potatoes. There must have been some confusion and instead of ending up at the lost property office, they finished up among some freight. Who knows?

We thanked the police profusely, and the poor old, muddled, much put-upon man. John had his coats and now we could fly home and relax. Well, not quite, because by now John had a bad cold, which is risky to fly with. If you've ever had a cold and flown somewhere, the earache can be unbearable. By the time we reached Karachi, I was seriously worried about John and hoped his eardrums would hold out at least until we got to Kuala Lumpur. I dreaded the thought of having to find medical treatment in Karachi.

We actually made it home in one piece and John still had functioning eardrums and his two coats, so all was well that ended well.

19

Robbed in Brussels

In November 1983, John and I spent three days in Brussels. This was part of a package deal offered by British Airways – for any trip taken to the UK, they added a three-day sojourn in a European capital of your choice, at no extra cost. Who could resist? We could have chosen Paris, Rome, Amsterdam or Frankfurt. I'd always had a soft spot for Brussels, though, with its mediaeval Grand Place, lace and chocolate shops and unique Flemish culture. John had never been there, so Brussels it was.

There we were, ensconced in the cosy little Hotel Grand Cloche, in the heart of Brussels. By the way, you can still stay at Grand Cloche: in fact, it's ranked among the top forty hotels in Brussels and offers good value for money. We'd go back there in a heartbeat if only we could afford to. I found it on the net and seeing it brought back lovely memories, with one exception.

On a chilly November Friday morning, Armistice Day, which in Belgium is a public holiday, we'd decided to take a train trip to Bruges. From looking at brochures, Bruges was an enchanting mediaeval town, with many original old buildings. It beckoned to us and so we set out for a brisk walk to the Terminal Midi, or Central Brussels railway station.

We were excited about our forthcoming trip and were chatting together, discussing what we might do in Bruges, when a group of dark-haired, rather scruffy children, between the ages of about eight to ten, ran up to us. We were caught completely off-guard and they zoomed in. They were collecting money for the poor, they told us.

'Oh, yes,' we replied, opening our wallets, but only planning to give them a few coins, 'let's see what we can find.'

They were laughing and chattering. In hindsight, probably laughing at us, the silly, seemingly rich tourists. Anyhow, we were sucked in.

'*Merci, monsieur*,' they called out, as they ran off down the cobbled street. 'You will go to heaven.'

It took us some time to process all this and at that stage we didn't realise we'd been robbed, in broad daylight, by a bunch of kids. It was not until we went to purchase our tickets to Bruges that, horror of horrors, there was no money. We'd had plenty that morning, having cashed some traveller's cheques at a Brussels bank the afternoon before, especially as we knew that Friday the eleventh was to be a public holiday. There were no international ATMs at that time.

'Have you got…?' we said to each other, and then trailed off when it dawned on us that those scruffy kids had taken our money for that day and both Diners Club cards as well. It was the most devastating, awful feeling.

A sympathetic man at the railway station said, 'I think you've been robbed by the gypsy kids. There's lots around here. You really have to watch out for them. They're bad news, real little criminals in the making.'

Well, yeah, now we knew.

To cut a long, sad story short, we spent the rest of the morning at the Brussels police headquarters. The police there were lovely to us and gave us coffee and plenty of chat, but it certainly wasn't the same as being in Bruges. A patrol car went looking for the culprits and they did succeed in rounding up some of them for us to identify.

'Yes,' we said, 'it's probably them, but we can't be sure, as the whole incident had happened so quickly and the kids look a bit different.'

The police told us that the children found ways to disguise themselves with hats or scarves, in order to make identification harder.

'They're trained well by their families,' the policeman added, 'and the crime continues through the generations.'

The good news was that we still had our passports and the rest of our travellers' cheques in John's money belt. As I'd already explained, we did lose both our Diners Club cards and spent a long, frustrating

Belgian police in the Grand Place, Brussels. We spent a morning at their headquarters, reporting the incident with the Gypsy kids.

time on a very bad phone line back in London, but were able to obtain new ones and continue our journey after only a couple of days.

By the time we left the Brussels police headquarters, we were absolutely starving and desperate for some lunch. We settled for some Hungarian goulash in a grubby, rather downmarket café, where no one else seemed to be dining.

'I bet we get food poisoning,' we said to each other, but at that stage, we felt so bad we just didn't care and the goulash was actually really delicious.

I couldn't believe that this had happened to us. After all, I particularly had visited Europe five times before. I'd always been wary and cautious and certainly had never been accosted. I felt really stupid. We both did.

The rest of that day we spent in the safety of our hotel room, getting stuck into the duty-free. After all, it's moments like these you need a good cognac, with chocolates, and Belgian ones are so delectable.

The whole incident brings to mind an old-English skipping rhyme that my mum used to recite to me: 'Beware of the gypsies in the woods'. It goes like this:

My mother said I never should play with the gypsies in the woods.

(Here, you could substitute play for talk – either way, you'd be much safer.)

And if I did, then she would say, you naughty girl to disobey
Your hair shan't curl
Your shoes won't shine
You naughty girl, you shan't be mine.
My father said that if I did, he'd bang my head with a teapot lid.

Apart from the last sentence which suggests child abuse, I think whoever wrote this was spot on. Don't talk to the gypsies at any cost, especially not on holidays. Actually, in view of recent events in Europe, I think that maybe the gypsies are the least of a traveller's problems. The moral of this story is to always be careful, but always have fun.

20

Jump on Those Scales and Ping That Girdle

I just adored holidaying in Europe and England, and, I believe, I always left a small part of me over there, but it was also wonderful and something of a relief to come back home safely to family and friends.

By the time dawn was breaking, the 747 was just reaching the north-western-most tip of Australia and you could look out the window, down to the red-orange earth below and gaze into a vast expanse of most of the time cloudless sky. You knew then you were home, although of course if you flew with Qantas, you were home as soon as you set foot in the plane. The accents of the cabin crew were comfortingly unmistakable. I think some of those who were less formal may have even said, 'G'day, luv. How are ya?'

A day or so later, it was time to go back to work and turn into a cabin crew member myself. Often, still jet-lagged and dizzy, the powers-that-be thought this an ideal time to see if you had your act together after a holiday. Time for a dreaded spot grooming check. Yep, it was a prime time to get caught out. Here's some of the things they checked.

Bar change. A float of five dollars was supposed to be carried in your work purse at all times, in change, not a single note. On the first morning back, many of us would shove a five-dollar note in and vow to ourselves to change it at the airport café.

First aid pack. This was expected to be filled with a correct number of items which of course had often not been replenished before we went on leave. Often we were missing a couple of aspirin, deltoid inhaler capsules (for ear trouble) or Band-Aids. We also carried bandages, but luckily no one ever haemorrhaged on my aircraft; it simply wasn't allowed. Of course, you could fill up once you found out there was a grooming check in progress, but it looked fishy and the checkie would be just as likely to request that we top up later, as she wanted to see it 'right now please'.

Stockings or pantyhose. On the first morning back, the only pair available were the ones you'd hastily removed before going on leave and of course they often had a ladder or hole that you hadn't noticed before. You therefore had to wear those, again vowing to buy a new pair at the airport and change. The mandatory spare pair also had a hole, but what the heck.

For various reasons that are too numerous to name, good intentions often didn't happen. The bar money didn't get changed, the first-aid kit wasn't topped up and the pantyhose didn't get purchased and you were sprung. Talk about living dangerously.

'What a bunch of slack tarts' was how the male flight crew used to refer to us, mostly in a jocular way.

The very best part of all, though, was the 'Jump on those scales and ping that girdle.' Yep, we were all expected to wear a girdle and, what's more, prove we were actually wearing it. I'm surprised that we didn't have to lift up our dresses, but that would have been a step too far, even in the 70s, However, we did have to grab the edge of this garment and make it go ping. Many of us used to wear elastic-topped pantyhose and pinged those instead, which usually worked.

Immediately after holidays was a key time for checking weight, as often careful diets would have gone out the window while we were on leave, as they tended to do, but it was sadistic, I think to check out our weight straight after holidays.

In all fairness, I must say Airlines of South Australia weren't quite as strict as some. They took the attitude that as long as you fitted in comfortably to your uniform and appeared to be in proportion with height and bone structure, then one or two extra kilos were OK. However, you were still expected to not stray too far from the ideal weights represented on charts, and I think most of us managed that. Naturally, I think it's fair enough for girls in our position, back then and today, to maintain a high standard of appearance; but not obsessively. There was one checkie who was super-thin herself; in fact, she had the figure of a praying mantis and she was quite paranoid about any amount of weight the rest of us gained, usually a pretty trivial amount. She made that quite apparent by making disapproving comments during weigh-ins.

There was one time, but I don't recall it being immediately after holidays, that the set of scales in the hostess lounge was broken and so the checkie (not the praying mantis) took a small group of us out to weigh on the baggage scales in the main terminal. This is absolutely true and was really humiliating; as the checkie thought it was OK to call out our weights. The traffic officers who were checking in passengers at the time were smirking, along with the passengers, and I felt like slapping them all and the checkie. I've also heard of this happening to another air hostess back in the 70s. Hopefully, public weigh-ins have now been outlawed along with any draconian rules regarding acceptable weight like those on silly height/weight charts.

I do hope the rules of today are a bit more realistic, though heaven knows there's lots of hype about diet and body consciousness. Too much, I think. Some months ago I flew to Sydney and one of the hostesses aboard was quite a bit heavier than would have been the norm when I was flying. However, she was attractive, friendly and seemed to be very good at her job. What's more, I'm sure she'd be able to fit through an emergency exit. I happen to be of the opinion that thinness doesn't always equate with healthiness. I'm more aware of this than many other people, having witnessed a close family member suffer for several years from the miseries of anorexia/bulimia.

Anyway, such were the delights of the spot grooming check, which after all went with the territory. I still wouldn't have missed out on any of the fun and drama for the world, despite it sometimes being very much like school.

21

Not For Sale, Ever

Tucked away in one of my bedroom drawers are a set of sheets. Not just any old sheets, but a set I bought in the mid-70s, from David Jones (yes, I once used to shop in upmarket department stores like David Jones, or DJs as it was usually known). The background of the sheets is white with well-known airlines written in colours of red, blue, green, black, yellow and even a splash of orange. Some of the airlines featured are no longer in existence, such as TAA, which was Trans Australia Airlines and was always in competition with my airline, Ansett Airlines of Australia; Pan-Am; TWA; UTA French Airlines, MAS (now operating separately as Malaysian and Singapore Airlines); and not forgetting our own Ansett Airlines, which was a part of my life for such a long time.

Other airlines that are still flying passengers around the world include British, KLM, Lufthansa, Cathay Pacific, Air New Zealand, JAL, Garuda and Olympic.

I get my sheets out every so often and they bring back so many memories of the travel variety; and I remember that I actually did fly with most of these airlines at some time or other: in fact, just about all except JAL, Cathay Pacific, UTA and Olympic.

Now, in case you were thinking of contacting me to try to acquire this museum piece, don't bother. Sorry, I didn't mean to be so blunt. They're mine and are going to remain so. No cajoling, blackmail or even offers of money will work. These sheets are special and are one of my few collector's items.

22

Sometimes It's Just the Little Things, Part 1

Some of the most memorable events of my flying career weren't spectacular enough to devote a whole chapter to, but they were nevertheless significant; maybe they were funny, which always made my day, or a bit scary, or even embarrassing, though not necessarily for me. Anyway, here's some I think you might enjoy. Sometimes I've changed a name, or perhaps not mentioned a name at all, in the interests of diplomacy, tact and not getting sued.

One morning, on the first flight of the day, Marg, a hostess, said the word 'shit', which reverberated loudly through the cabin, causing some raised eyebrows. She apparently hadn't realised the PA system was still switched on, and in the 70s, the 's' word was still a no-no and frowned upon, especially from an air hostess. Of course someone reported her and she was in trouble, but we all thought it was pretty funny. I can't remember why she said 'shit', not that it matters. I imagine that she received a dressing down from management by way of punishment.

I also recall Captain Bob's aborted landing into Whyalla. The weather was particularly horrible on this afternoon flight to beautiful downtown Whyalla, which we all thought was a bit of a hole. It was very industrial, and we were experiencing crosswinds, which of course can be dangerous for aircraft. Just before we were about to land, the engines made a horrible grinding, accelerating noise, which was really very scary. We found we were climbing again.

Captain Bob, who was an ex-RAAF man and a top-notch pilot, but was also a real character and much loved by all his workmates, especially the hostesses, came over the PA. He said something like 'Sorry about that, everyone, but if we'd attempted to land, we'd have been spread all over the runway by now like raspberry jam. Didn't think you'd want that, so we'll try again. We may have to turn back to Adelaide.'

I can't remember whether we ended up returning to Adelaide, but Captain Bob's jocular manner reassured everyone. Many of the passengers were regulars and quite familiar with Bob's style on the PA, which was unique to Bob and very Australian. He was such fun and a lovely man.

While on the subject of Captain Bob, whenever a new air hostess started with ASA and flew with him, he'd scribble his phone number on his hand, show it to the new girl and say, 'Call this number, and if a woman answers, hang up.' Whereupon he'd crack up laughing. We all got his joke and I'm pretty sure that no one ever phoned. He was extremely loyal to his wife and family, which is something that can't be said about all the pilots. I did hear, on the gossip grapevine that once, a group of hostesses turned up at Captain Bob's door wearing negligées and when he answered the door, told him they wanted to accept his invitation. It was a practical joke and fortunately Bob took it as such.

Another time, a few years later, we had to abort a take-off at Adelaide Airport at night. The captain, not Bob this time, explained that another aircraft had been on the runway. That was a close call. Aborted take-offs and landings are very unsettling.

Shortly after I'd started with ASA, there was one particular captain, Ron, who thought it very amusing to commence the take-off roll before the senior had time to get back to her seat. The hostess seats were at the rear of the Fokker 27, but if there were seats available in the cabin, the junior was expected to take one of those. Anyway, once the cabin was prepared and ready for take-off, the senior went to the flight compartment to inform the crew that we were ready to roll. The pilots would wait until the senior was safely seated, except Ron. He was also an ex-RAAF pilot and very competent; however, some of these blokes flew by their own rule book. He went hurtling down the runway while the poor senior was forced to race back to her seat in a very undignified manner. He thought it was hilarious, until several of us reported his dangerous behaviour and then it soon stopped. We got the impression that captains could do whatever they damn well liked and get away with it; and they did.

You've no doubt heard of the saying 'grabbing the cat by the tail'. Well, I literally did on one flight to Whyalla. In fact, we'd landed at Whyalla and the loaders were busy taking luggage from out of the baggage compartment. I'd been saying goodbyes to passengers, when I became aware of scratching and meowing coming from a pet pack which had yet to be unloaded. There was one grumpy, unhappy and very large ginger cat trying to escape from its pet pack. In fact, it was already three-quarters of the way out and, just in time, I swooped down and managed to grab its tail and hang on fast. I had to continue holding on for some time before the loader became aware and was able to help me get it back into its box and somehow temporarily secure it. I don't think I could have held it much longer and of course it was yowling and making a terrible racket. Miraculously, it didn't scratch or pee on me, as you might imagine a nervous, upset cat would do. Anyhow, I did prevent it from running over into the scrubland around the Whyalla airport to join the feral cats and possums, which I'm sure it wouldn't have liked much. Come to think of it, the pet owners wouldn't have been too happy either.

One event that I didn't witness first-hand, but heard from a reliable source, was after evening flights one night, several crews went to the airport club, which was really just a bar for airline staff at the end of a long day. Lots of people drank themselves under the table at the club and they used to brag about it at work the next day. This activity was never my style and while I enjoy a couple of drinks, especially bubbly, as much as the next person, I never wanted to drink so much that I'd get into awkward or embarrassing situations.

Anyway, at some stage during this particular evening, two hostesses, who had a crush on a particular first officer, had a real down-on-the-floor physical catfight over this bloke. The fact that he was married to someone else, and I think may even have had a small child, didn't bother them at all. No doubt, too much alcohol played a part; however, knowing the people concerned in this little drama, I could believe it. Just wish I'd been a fly on the wall.

One of my special moments was working in the cabin and serving tea and biscuits to the reigning Miss South Australia at the time, which was about 1975 or 1976, and to her chaperone. The Miss South Australia Quest was a big deal in those days and they raised lots of money for what was then known as the Spastic Centre, now called SCOSA. Each state in Australia had a similar competition yearly and the state finalists went on to the national final, where Miss Australia was crowned. They always claimed it wasn't a beauty contest, and to some extent that was true, but certainly looks, personality and poise were important, as well as general knowledge. However, it mostly raised funds and awareness of the children in centres around Australia.

Anyway, on this particular day, I was talking briefly with Miss SA and she and her chaperone asked whether I might seriously consider joining the next Miss SA Quest. They both thought I'd be a good candidate and I replied graciously that I would go home and give it some thought. I was so flattered and, yes, it was very special to me that someone thought I had the necessary qualities. I didn't ever enter, as some years previously, before I started flying, I was in the Adelaide Children's Hospital Girl of the Year quest. It was an enjoyable experience, but something I only wanted to do once. Interestingly enough, I won a money-raiser prize and was one of two girls awarded a place at an air hostess academy in Adelaide: A little like a modelling/finishing school, I guess. I didn't go, which I now regret, because I was then accepted for ASA and time got away with me.

23

Sometimes It's Just the Little Things, Part 2

One of the funniest things that ever happened was our good Captain Phil using the aircraft loo, between flights, to supposedly save himself time instead of walking over to the Adelaide terminal. In between flights, the aircraft was of course cleaned, new catering put on board and the toilet pan removed for emptying. Well, along came Phil, who didn't realize that the pan had just been removed. The loo on the F27 was right at the back. My co-hostess Ellen and I were in the back seats, having completed our duties, and were chatting before the next flight. Presently we heard the sound of a really loud tinkle, tinkle hitting the ground below. Poor old Phil was peeing directly onto the tarmac. Ellen and I cracked up laughing and one of the loaders, standing by the back door, was also aware of what was happening and he joined in. We were all nearly bent double, but after a few minutes, Phil emerged red-faced and furious. I suppose I could say really pissed off. The three of us tried to stop laughing; we dared not look at each other. Phil straightened himself up, puffed out his chest and, ignoring us, went trotting off down the aircraft stairs. I can only imagine how embarrassed he was, but of course we started laughing again until it was time for the passengers to board.

On a return flight from Whyalla one day, our captain received a message that there was a bomb aboard our aircraft. Of all our outports, Whyalla would have been the most likely for this to happen, as it had, let's say, an assorted population, and some of them were considered dodgy. I wasn't flying senior at the time, so it's hard to recall what information exactly we passed on to passengers, but the other hostess and I did have to search drawers, cupboards, the loo and so on. This was an unnerving feeling. Turns out, it was a hoax call and we landed quite safely, but it makes you wonder about the mentality of people who do that.

Captain Gil was a great bloke; friendly, good at his job but easy-going, and very good-looking. If he was on the sign-on sheet for your flight, you knew it was going to be a good day. Sound good so far? He had just one flaw, and that was that he never stopped talking to draw breath, even when he was eating. On days where we spent all day at an out-port, such as Mount Gambier or Kangaroo Island, the four crew would often eat together in whatever hotel we were in. Captain Gil talked and ate, and ate and talked, while the rest of us barely got a word in and had a good view of the food mashing up in Gil's mouth. It was a bit off-putting while trying to enjoy your own food. My friend Di used to call him the Mixmaster.

We often had Aboriginal people on board, as many of them lived in towns like Port Lincoln and Ceduna, on South Australia's west coast. They sometimes had a reputation for being drunk and disorderly, which was unfair, as many white passengers were drunk and behaved in a far worse way. I was fortunate enough to have had very few of the troublesome variety of either race. Bad behaviour on my flights was simply not allowed. Anyway, I always found the Aboriginal people very affable, with a great sense of fun and humour, but yes, sometimes they were tipsy.

One elderly Aboriginal man, upon disembarking into Adelaide from Ceduna, lunged towards me at the bottom of the stairs, saying, 'I wanna kiss from you.'

Thinking quickly, I took a step back and said primly, 'It's against the rules to kiss the passengers, so I'll just wave you goodbye.'

He ambled off towards the terminal quite happily.

Yet another of our Aboriginal passengers sang 'Mull of Kintyre' from Port Lincoln to Adelaide, although he fell asleep about five minutes before landing. It was really very entertaining and funny. Julie my co-hostess and I had a good laugh and a fun flight. I can never hear 'Mull of Kintyre' without thinking of that bloke.

My favourite story about Aboriginal passengers is this. Around the mid-70s, I had medium-length brunette hair that curled under around my face, with a full fringe. I think it was a pageboy bob. I also used to wear quite a lot of eye make-up, namely green eye shadow and black mascara and liner and probably brightish lipstick. Anyhow, on this particular evening, it was my turn to do the cabin demo, but the other hostess was serving in the cabin.

When she reached these two young Aboriginal lads to take their order, they asked, 'Where's Cleopatra?'

'Who?' asked my co-hostess?

'You know, Cleopatra, the other girl. Can she come out?'

I don't remember what the other hostess said, probably just explained that we had a system of working we had to stick to and couldn't change it halfway. Whatever she said, I was always quite flattered and amused by their request. You can see what I mean when I said they had a unique sense of humour. So cute.

One weekend, Airlines of South Australia took a charter flight of tourists to Alice Springs for the weekend. En route, we stopped at Birdsville, on the Queensland/South Australian border. The Birdsville Hotel is an iconic watering hole and our passengers were keen to visit the hotel and of course have a drink there. We joined them, but of course being on duty we had Cokes or lemon squash. One of the town characters said he'd give us a tour of Birdsville, which really just consists of a main street. So we got into his car, all four of us, and were treated to a mini motorcade along Birdsville's main street. I think he was quite proud of doing this and probably shared his story over a few drinks at the Birdsville pub, which, by the way, is a very attractive historical building.

I'm afraid the Alice trip didn't end well for me or my co-hostess Julie, as we'd decided to eat a prawn cocktail for an entrée at dinner that evening. This was in 1975, before tourist facilities were upgraded and before the advent of Uluru and the high-end resort. It was extremely unwise to have had prawns in Australia's Red Centre in those days. It was, after all, a long way from the sea and prawn trawlers. We both got very sick, but fortunately not until we got home on the Sunday evening. We both avoided prawns for a very long time after that.

One of the highlights of my flying days was my trip to Sydney on the flight deck of a Boeing 727-200 (the stretched 727). I was on holidays, but the flight was chock-a-block and so the traffic officer, passenger service officer as they're known today, asked the captain whether I would be permitted to ride in the extra crew seat behind the captain. He very kindly agreed and so I had the best ride ever. Up front, I really felt like I was flying. I had dinner there too, although naturally no alcohol was allowed. The Adelaide to Sydney flight is about one and a half hours and passes over a good deal of barren landscape. However, it was at night so, as I looked 30,000 feet down, I could see faint lights of the small country towns and even lightning, which was some distance away. The best part was landing in Sydney, with the runway lit up right in front of me and the roar of the jet engines louder than in the cabin. It really was an incredible experience.

I simply can't resist relating this story. Airlines of South Australia used to have intakes of trainee first officers from Melbourne. As you can imagine, some of the girls used to go ape over these blokes and some very bad behaviour went on, as I told you in the previous chapter. Remember the two girls fighting over the married first officer? I heard about this other incident from a reliable source, as it didn't happen on my flight. One of our hostesses was married to a training captain and they were both rostered for the same flight on this particular day. She went up to the flight compartment that morning to take the tea/coffee orders and get ETA, weather reports, and so on.

When she'd gone, the brash young first officer, who wasn't very impressed, turned to his trainer captain and said. 'Fancy waking up to that every morning!'

To which his trainer replied, 'I do, actually. She's my wife.'

If ever there was a hole in the ground moment for the FO, that was it. I never heard how the first officer's relationship with his trainer proceeded after that little gaffe. I would love to know.

I can't resist telling this one either. We were always encouraged to chat to the passengers if we had the time and it could be very pleasant to find someone to talk to, rather than just moving up and down the cabin, seemingly aloof. However, we had one girl who took this to a whole new level. Janene (not her real name), would stop and chat to people, on a fully loaded flight, with tail winds, which cut down on cabin service time. It was hurry, hurry, all the way. The co-hostess would have to go out to the cabin and point out, diplomatically, that she needed to get a move on, as we'd be landing shortly. Once, I think, the wheels were almost on the ground and I had to unstrap from my seat, grab her and make her sit down. She seemed almost unaware of the situation, so immersed was she in the conversation.

On another day, I was flying with Janene to Kangaroo Island. It was a cold blustery night and we were glad to shut the doors and warm the cabin. One of our passengers on that evening was a TV personality of the day, who I'll call Gaynor. She was wearing a real fur coat, which horrified me. Even back in the 70s, people were starting to react negatively to the wearing of real fur coats and rightly so.

Janene whispered to me, 'Have you seen Gaynor's coat? Isn't it gorgeous? Have we got somewhere special we can hang it up, maybe?'

I should explain here that on the F27s we just had luggage racks, not overhead lockers like today.

I felt strongly about the wearing of real fur and I snapped back, 'She should be ashamed of herself. You can find somewhere else to put it and give her the star treatment if you want, but I'm not.' I know my feelings were coloured by the dislike I felt for Gaynor, as I found her snobbish and attention-seeking.

Janene looked at me as if I'd just slapped her and went off to gush to Gaynor about her gorgeous coat. I quite liked Janene; she was pleasant enough to work with, but it sometimes seemed as if she was on another planet.

24

Things on Planes That Go Bump in the Night

In May 1977, I took off on holiday again for my second trip to America. I flew from Sydney to Honolulu and from there to San Francisco. I was going to visit friends in Indiana, Kansas and Oregon. There had been the threat of an air traffic control strike that very week, but luckily I flew out of Sydney without anything disastrous happening. I heard that the following week they did go out, which would have messed up my plans, and no doubt others' too.

Anyway, I boarded the Qantas 747 with a deep sigh of relief. Airline staff were always subject to load and I didn't see many vacant seats. I'd made it and was enjoying a pre-dinner drink and chatting to the two Brisbane-based Ansett hostesses next to me. After dinner, we all settled back to watch a movie – I wish I could remember what it was. In those days, as I said earlier, they used to show the in-flight movie on a large screen against the bulkheads in certain sections of the cabin. I wish they still did it that way. I'm not a fan of those squinty little screens installed in the backs of seats; especially if the annoying person in front of you wants to lie right back.

It was going to be a long haul. Sydney to Honolulu was ten hours back then. By now, the sky outside had darkened. I don't remember there being a moon and below us an inky-black Pacific Ocean stretched for thousand of kilometres.

For some time, the flight was smooth; the aircraft flew serenely through the night and the soft hypnotic hum of Rolls Royce engines was soporific. The cabin lights were dimmed and people started to doze off. Before long, though, we started to hit some turbulence, just niggly at first, and then all hell broke loose. Lightning flashed menacingly outside the windows and our 747 lurched about violently. It's amazing how something as massive as a 747 can be at the mercy of the forces of nature.

All of a sudden, without warning, we dropped like a stone. I've never experienced a tummy-taker like that one before or since. Remember how, as a child, you'd be delighted when the family car hit a road hump and seemed to almost fly? Remember the weird, quite exhilarating feeling in the pit of your stomach? That's a tummy-taker. This one was mega, though, and more scary than exhilarating. All of a sudden, overhead lockers were coming open and people's duty-free goods, clothes and briefcases were airborne around the cabin. Some passengers were holding their hands protectively over their heads to avoid the flying missiles, and some were screaming.

Until this event, I'd never, ever been afraid of flying, but even I was wondering what it would be like to ditch into the Pacific Ocean in the middle of the night. It was not a thought I wanted to dwell on and I felt just as frightened as everyone else. Fortunately, I'd had my seat belt loosely fastened and quickly tightened it when the turbulence got nasty, so I didn't rise up out of my seat and injure myself as some did.

The storm seemed to go on for ages, but finally abated. The captain gave us a reassuring address, but told us that we might have to change planes in Honolulu. Cabin crew came around to check on passengers and tend to those who had been injured.

On the ground in Honolulu, where thankfully it was daylight once again, I discovered we'd been struck by lightning and that the aircraft needed to be thoroughly checked out, as a result of which our arrival into San Francisco would be delayed. Several people had to be taken to hospital in Honolulu as they had suffered concussion and others had severe cuts and bruises. I also learned that we'd dropped over a thousand feet in a few seconds, a tummy-taker and a half.

In the end, Qantas paid for us to stay overnight in San Francisco, after having changed over to an alternative aircraft as, by the time we arrived there, we were too late to make connecting flights. Even airline staff like me were given a free room for the night at one of the San Francisco Airport motels.

I phoned my friends in Indiana to tell them about the drama and my subsequent late arrival. Of course, they were glad I was safe, but were quite excited to hear about the storm and got me to relate the story to many of their friends. We dined out on the incident for several days. After spending the night in San Francisco, everything fell into place and went smoothly.

Today, of course, you will be told in the pre-flight PA to keep your seat belt loosely fastened when seated. This advisory originates from that Qantas flight on a stormy evening in May 1977, and no doubt from other incidences of which I'm not aware. So I am a part of airline history and not just on the basis of having flown with Ansett Airlines of South Australia. This incident was discussed for some years at our emergency revalidation sessions. I wonder whether it still is?

25

Coming to America and Canada Too

You may or may not know that the title of this chapter (except for 'and Canada too'), belongs to both a well-known movie starring Eddie Murphy, and an equally well-known popular song by Neil Diamond. I'm a fan of both the movie and the song, so I'm going to borrow 'Coming to America'.

After having travelled to England and Europe in 1974, I was well and truly ready to see America and Canada. I was fortunate to have met several Americans and Canadians on my travels, who'd had no hesitation in inviting me to stay with them when I visited, so that's just what I did. Looking back, I suppose that could have been risky and I can honestly say I'm not sure whether I'd be as game today, nor would I recommend that others do so.

The two friends in Vancouver I'd met on my twelve-day Cosmos tour of Europe and so I'd had the chance to get to know them quite well. The lady I was to stay with in Lake Oswego, Oregon, I met on a bus tour to Canterbury in England and she appeared to be pleasant and genuine, as did the friend she was with. I struck up a conversation with them in an old-fashioned sweet shop in Canterbury. My Indiana contact was a bloke a few years older than me who I met in Westminster Abbey, as you do. My Canadian friend from Toronto was a bloke I'd met on my 1973 bus tour of New Zealand, so likewise I'd got to know him fairly well too. I considered myself a fairly good judge of character, even at twenty-three. So off I went without any qualms. Well, to be completely honest, I wasn't entirely sure that I should have agreed to go to Indiana to see Harold, but that all got sorted out as, by the time I arrived, he'd found some of his friends for me to stay with and I hardly saw him. I think he'd lost interest, which suited me fine. I just loved his friends Bonnie and Gene, though.

Once again, I waited nervously at the check-in desk in Sydney to see whether I was on or off. Would you believe that I scored the very last seat on the Boeing 707 to Vancouver? New South Wales had just begun their end-of-first-term school holidays, so there were heaps of families flying to Fiji and Tahiti, which were our two ports of call en route to Vancouver. I remember having to run to board the aircraft, which seemed miles away. Down one corridor, then another, a bit like a bad dream. I plonked down in my seat, flushed and rather breathless, with barely time to do up my seat belt. I was a bit surprised at Qantas operating the Boeing 707 for this flight and not the much larger Boeing 747, as it was the beginning of school holidays and a long-distance across the Pacific. I wasn't quite so enchanted with the 707 this time.

At Nadi in Fiji, we landed at sunset, which was beautiful; rich shades of orange, pink and purple lit up the clouds outside the aircraft windows and highlighted the swaying palm trees. As we took off again, I could see the picture-perfect beach and thought to myself how nice Fiji would be for a holiday. Would you believe that I still haven't been there? It's so close to Australia too, but never say never; I, or rather we, still might make it. Just that I won't appear young and glamorous on the beach any more, but I guess you can't have everything. The following hours were all in darkness and we disembarked for an hour or so in Papeete at the unearthly hour of two a.m. Most long-distance flights from Australia involve unearthly hours at some stage.

We landed into Vancouver at around seven a.m., I think. It's weird crossing the International Date Line. I had to keep reminding myself that we were a day or maybe over half a day behind Australia. It was rather confusing.

I stayed in Vancouver for that day and night with my friend Leslie and her husband Glenn, who was a newspaper photographer. I just loved Vancouver with its forests, mountains and its close proximity to the sea. In future years, it would make me think of New Zealand, but that chapter is still to be told. Leslie and I took her gorgeous setter dog Raifiki for a walk and I enjoyed the lush gardens and the chilly spring air. I remember the sound of running water too; I can't recall whether there was a creek nearby but there must have been.

The weather in the Pacific north-west was quite cold until I reached California. The next morning, I boarded the bus to Portland, Oregon, but remember feeling so happy that I was to return to Vancouver for my last week, as I'd already fallen in love with it and I liked Leslie and Kathy a great deal, as they were friendly, welcoming and fun to be with. In those days there was no Facebook or email and so over the years we've lost touch. How lovely it would be to talk to them today.

The bus journey to Portland was a twelve-hour jaunt, but provided me with a good look at the Pacific north-west region, which I'll always have a soft spot for. I was captivated by the snow-capped Cascades and the forests and little towns like Tacoma, Bellingham and Everett. Of course I passed through Seattle as well, with its eye-catching Space Needle tower and volcanic Mount Ranier a spectacular backdrop.

The only slightly unnerving thing to happen was a tall guy wearing a cowboy hat, who kept eyeing me off and grinning. I only became aware of it as I'd struck up a conversation with a woman who lived not far from my friend in Lake Oswego. She nudged me and whispered, 'That guy is giving you the eye.'

He was quite good-looking, but I thought rather smooth and cocky. Travelling alone, I certainly wasn't about to engage in conversation. He actually made me feel very uncomfortable. I've since thought that he strongly resembled that serial killer Ted Bundy who I know was in the Washington State area of the US around 1975. It's too creepy and unpleasant even to contemplate.

I arrived in Portland at about seven p.m., met my friends, forgot all about Mr Cowboy Hat and over the next week I had a really good look at the Pacific north-west, which was my introduction to that massive country, the United States of America.

26

Oregon With Ryllis and Charlie

Ryllis and Charlie were my wonderful hosts in Lake Oswego, Oregon. Right from the moment I stepped off the Greyhound bus in Portland, after my twelve-hour journey, they treated me like a daughter. Ryllis and Charlie had two adult sons, so I think that Ryllis enjoyed setting up a girlie bedroom for me. There was a pretty quilt on the bed and fresh flowers in the room; even a radio, which I tuned in to the pop music station. I clearly recall Elton John singing 'Philadelphia Freedom' at the time. I still love that song. Likewise 'The Hustle' (we were right in the disco music era) by Van McCoy and the Soul City Symphony, 'Magic' by Pilot and 'Please Mr Postman' from the Carpenters.

You may remember me mentioning that I'd met Ryllis on a day tour of Canterbury in England the year before. We'd both been into an old fashioned lolly shop there and exchanged sweets and then conversation. I told her I was an air hostess and that was how she came to invite me to her house in Oregon.

Lake Oswego was a quiet and pretty suburb not far from Portland and, like Vancouver, had lush gardens as a result of good rainfall. Luckily for me, although the weather was cool, I don't remember any rain. Being May, it was springtime in the US and, as we drove towards the mountains one day, there were apple orchards in full bloom. Further up, we reached the snowline and all of a sudden it was winter, and skiers in bright colours were everywhere. Ryllis took a photo of me with two of them and, although they were very obliging, I had the feeling they just wanted to get on with their afternoon of skiing. I imagined that people living here would have been skiing since they

Canterbury, where I met Ryllis.

were toddlers. I felt a tinge of envy, as I'd never been skiing and am not particularly athletic.

I later found out that we had been on Mount Hood, which is a dormant volcano and in the same range as Mount St Helens. Later, I was to stand on the slopes of other volcanoes, in Bali and New Zealand, but Mount Hood was my first. I'm thankful that it remained dormant.

Further down the mountain, we stopped by the upper reaches of the Columbia River, which was flowing fast and tumbling over rocks still wearing patches of snow. I had my photo taken sitting on one of the rocks. It shows a much younger me, dipping my fingers into the water, which not surprisingly was icy cold.

I was continually surprised by the friendliness and warmth of the American people. I was amused that they enjoyed hearing me speak. I didn't think I had an accent and I was more interested in hearing them talk.

My friend Ryllis was a secretary at the local high school and she took me to school with her one day, where I was certainly a curiosity, but in the nicest possible way. At the school, I was invited to sit in on a history lesson, which I'm sorry to say I remember nothing about. I also ate lunch in the canteen, quite unlike anything Australian schools had, and spoke with many of the kids. This experience was oddly surreal and yet was

Me, pretending to play golf and to know what I'm doing.

exactly like the way US high schools are portrayed on TV and movies. I really did feel I'd walked onto a TV set. The social structure was the same: the pretty and popular cheerleader girls and jocks; the middle-of-the-road kids, neither one thing or the other; and the not-smart-and-not-pretty-either group, usually to be ignored. I wonder whether it's worse today with social media. I believe it is, poor kids.

I also visited Ryllis's friend Mrs Fleischmann, who was a teacher of an elementary class. These kids were adorable seven and eight-year-olds and we had a lovely, fun hour of questions and answers. The children asked me about Australia and I in turn asked them about America.

One day, Ryllis took me down the Pacific coast road to Cannon Beach, where there's a famous landmark called Haystack Rock. The Pacific coast is especially breathtaking, whatever side of the Pacific you happen to be on. In Sydney and in New Zealand, it's always dramatically beautiful. Anyway, at Cannon Beach, Ryllis and I visited a bakery famous for its Haystack Loaf. I looked the bakery up online to see whether it was still there and sure enough, it was, I mean is. It's a well-established business that began in 1911. They had a little coffee shop set up inside the bakery and Ryllis and I had coffee and a piece of pecan pie: yum. That was another first for me. We also bought a loaf of the Haystack bread and, yes, it was delicious. Just down the street was a small boutique, which in those days I could never resist. I saw a shirt. It had a white background and embroidered in yellow, red and green, and black were names of American cities. There was San Francisco, Los Angeles, Chicago and New York. I had to have that shirt. Ryllis likewise decided to buy one the same and we said we'd think of each other whenever we wore it. I still have the shirt with its large white 70s collar; and you know, I'd still wear it if only it would fit, which it sadly doesn't.

Before I head off to San Francisco, I simply must tell you about the funniest incident of my week there. Well, trying to play golf with Ryllis was funny, mostly because I was so bad, but it's also embarrassing and, I must admit, boring. Golf isn't my thing at all, but of course I wanted to be polite and give it a go. Anyway, one evening, before I was to leave, Ryllis organised with her younger son Mike, who was a cadet cop, and his friend to take me out to a bluegrass tavern for a few drinks. We were chatting, and then suddenly I smelt something unfamiliar.

'I think there's something burning in here,' I said, all innocence. 'I wonder what it could be?'

Both Mike and his friend looked at me as if I'd migrated from Mars and asked, 'Haven't you ever smelt grass before?'

'Grass? You mean…'

'Yeah, we mean dope.'

I'd really never had anything to do with weed/grass/whatever in my life. No one in my circle back home smoked it and it certainly would have been frowned on. I felt a little foolish, naïve and not very sophisticated any more; not that I wanted to smoke dope of course.

I flew out of Portland to San Francisco with Western Airlines. (Western merged with Delta in 1987). I was by myself now and felt a bit lonely after having had company all week. Still, San Francisco was all I'd imagined it to be and more. Everything in America seemed larger than life and I was soaking it up like a sponge.

27

Postcards from America

I was going to name this chapter 'Just an Old-fashioned Slide Show' but, in this digital age, it occurred to me that many people wouldn't know what I was talking about. Thankfully, postcards are still available. They must be, as I've seen them in shops, so here's a description of some of my favourites. I've also included some of my own photos.

Sunset over Fiji, just the way I described it in 'Coming to America'. Brilliant pink/orange skies silhouetting the palm trees. This view soon vanished out of sight, however, as my plane was ascending rapidly en route to Vancouver, and unfortunately I didn't have a window seat.

Lions Gate Bridge in West Vancouver, British Columbia. I remember crossing that bridge on several occasions with my friend Kathy. Spread out below is Vancouver Harbour, part of the city, and high, snow-capped peaks rising up behind. What a gorgeous place. How lovely it would be to have a holiday house here.

A magnificent hollow tree in Stanley Park, Vancouver. Found along one of the forest trails, this particular tree was apparently huge enough to hold a parked car. The forest path looks quiet and inviting and was obviously taken during autumn, judging by the red and gold leaves.

A view of the sea-facing Sylvia Hotel, where I discoed until two in the morning of my departure from Canada; the flight left at seven a.m. I remember dancing the night away to songs like Gloria Gaynor's 'Never Can Say Goodbye', Linda Ronstadt's 'When Will I Be Loved' and 'The Hustle' by Van McCoy and the Soul City Symphony. Outside, the lights of the harbour twinkled while I danced on. Hard to believe that I once had that much energy.

Moving along to the Oregon coast, with its wild waves, white caps and spectacular rock formations, among them Haystack Rock. Here too, blue/purple hills nearby rise high over the scene.

Everybody get ready to laugh now. Here's a photo of me holding a golf club and pretending I know what to do with it. I am the least sporty person imaginable and I was hopeless at golf. I kept getting distracted by the distant snow-capped Cascades, but I couldn't help myself, as the scenery in the north-west Pacific always took my breath away.

The ski lift at Mount Hood, Oregon. This is on the slopes of a volcano (dormant, thankfully). Masses of snow are to be seen, as there was on the day my friends took me up there, and skiers in their bright coloured outfits were whooshing around me. I was quite envious of them.

The Golden Gate Bridge. My photo shows vehicles just rounding the corner of a hill and onto the road that crosses over this spectacular bridge. I was so lucky on that weekend. The sun shone continually and there was not a patch of fog or smog to be seen. Apparently, people can go days on end without getting a glimpse of the bridge.

Busy Union Square in San Francisco on a Saturday morning, with those wonderful rattly trams, lots of people and stylish shops all under a brilliant Californian spring sun.

San Francisco Airport showing an American Airlines McDonnell Douglas DC10 aircraft, which they dubbed the Luxury Liner, that was to take me to Indianapolis. The DC10s were beautiful aircraft, streamlined and elegant and it's a shame that they had to discontinue using them on passenger routes. The reason was issues with the cargo doors, from which several tragic accidents resulted. The DC10s were converted to cargo planes.

Me, in the lounge room at Bonnie and Gene's, my friends in Lafayette, Indiana. I seemed to be laughing, but I did have fun there and we were often laughing or giggling about something, fuelled by Harvey Wallbangers, which then became my favourite drink of the moment.

Me again, this time climbing into Bonnie and Gene's car for my return flight to Indianapolis and on to Toronto. Their car seemed so big, but then everyone else there seemed to have massive cars too. Real gas-guzzlers.

Toronto International Airport, taken at night. I arrived in the afternoon, so this is a postcard. It looks impressive and vast, but I can only imagine the way it is now. The sun is setting in the west, night lights have appeared, and some distant tails of Air Canada planes are visible.

28

Sunny San Francisco

Unfortunately, I only spent a few days in San Francisco, but it was enough time for me to experience its vibe, do a little shopping and see a few sights. Certainly I would love to make a return visit. Sadly, that hasn't happened and, although I did make an overnight stop in San Francisco in 1977, due to mechanical trouble with our plane which was caused by a bad storm, which I've told you about, it probably doesn't count.

Unfortunate too is that I don't remember a great deal, but do recall the vibrancy and colour of the city and the glorious spring sunshine that weekend. San Francisco didn't seem as big as I'd expected; certainly not overwhelmingly huge like London the year before. However, it was an American city and therefore an unknown quantity to me, and it was a little unnerving being there alone.

I recall that I stayed three nights in the Sir Francis Drake Hotel, just a short distance from Union Square. The doormen wore Beefeater costumes and they still do – I checked on the net.

I made a beeline for Union Square and walked a few blocks just soaking in the atmosphere and the sun. Weather in the Pacific northwest had been quite cold, but here it was just what you imagine California weather to be, warm and sunshiny. After walking a few blocks, thinking I was being terribly adventurous, I became anxious about getting lost and so I wheeled around and made my way back to the shopping area where I felt at ease. I've always enjoyed people-watching; seeing what people were wearing and who they were with. San Francisco didn't disappoint. The young girls all seemed to be pretty, yet casual, and the African-American men were dapper and looked as if they'd just stepped out of a disco. One bloke in particular stood out. He was very tall and dressed all in white, including his hat. He spread out his arms as he approached me and said something, but I didn't catch it. I took off like a frightened rabbit. He was probably harmless; maybe he was my guardian angel in disguise or maybe not. I don't know if they had a drug dealer on every street corner back then, so maybe he was one of those. I'll never know. I also noticed a few hippie leftovers from the late 60s.

I think I may have stopped for some morning tea then: an ice cream or coffee and an egg salad sandwich, to which I was fast becoming addicted. The Americans did them so well and I was always bowled over by the serving sizes. The sandwich was sort of like a club sandwich and had potato chips on the side as well as salad. Did I scoff the lot? I think I probably did as those were the days when it was oh so easy to shed a few extra pounds/kilos quickly. Sigh.

By now I was eager to make my way to the I. Magnin department store. I. Magnins had been recommended to me by my friend Ryllis and it was quite an icon in San Francisco at the time. It had been started by a woman called Mary-Ann Magnin back in 1876 who named it after her husband Isaac. They started out selling lotions and exclusive clothing for babies, but then expanded into high fashion from Paris. In 1975 there were also I. Magnin stores in Portland, Phoenix and Chicago. The store was high-end and sophisticated and it didn't take long for me to find the front doors, where I dived in and spent a few hours doing what I did best back then – shopping.

I bought, among other things, a gorgeous dress. It was navy-blue with white pin spots, and had a square neck with tucks and white stitching on the short sleeves. It was pretty, feminine and summery, but chic. The I. Magnins assistant boxed it up beautifully for me and even tied the parcel with a bow. I floated outside on a cloud, head held high, clutching my I. Magnins box and feeling like a movie star. I must admit, though, that movie stars usually exit a shop with multiple bags and boxes. However, I was very happy with my one.

The weather the next day, Sunday, was just as glorious as the day before and I thought it a good idea to take myself on a day tour of San Francisco, so that at least I'd be able to say that I'd seen some of the important sights. The bus took us to Muir Woods, the magnificent Redwood forest. The trees seemed to rise up forever and cast a shady canopy over the park. Until visiting New Zealand's Bay of Islands recently, I've never seen anything to rival those trees for sheer height. They were certainly beautiful. I love trees. We then left the Muir Woods and drove around the hilly areas just out of the city and suburbs and I experienced a moment of homesickness when the coach driver pointed out some eucalypts, which I could also smell in the warm breeze. The driver also pointed out a house where Greta Garbo the movie star had lived. It was certainly isolated enough for her wanting-to-be-alone moments. He then drove us to a section of the San Andreas Fault, but it was best not to dwell on the consequences of that splitting open. These memories are a bit sketchy, as it's quite a long time since 1975.

Lastly we saw the Golden Gate Bridge impressively spanning Oakland Bay. We then made a short stop in Sausalito, the artist's colony where there were some very expensive homes, especially the ones overlooking the bay. I have a print of San Francisco on the wall of my lounge, which I think may have come from a shop there.

It would have been great to have finished my brief stay in San Francisco with a drink at the top of Nob Hill or a meal on Fisherman's Wharf, but I didn't feel confident enough to do that alone. I felt that would keep for a day when I had some company, and of course, as I've already said, that hasn't happened. However, I have so many special memories that I don't feel I can complain.

The following day, it was time to move on to Indiana, so I made my way to the San Francisco airport and headed to the American Airlines check-in desk, where I had no trouble whatsoever in being checked in and issued with a seat number. It was a window seat, which I always requested, and the American Airlines staff were pleasant and friendly. I remember, while waiting for my flight to board, I heard a pager announcement for Paul and Linda McCartney, which was exciting, even though I didn't see them. It just had to be them, the former Beatle and his wife. They were most likely in San Francisco to perform with their band Wings, of whom I was a fan.

The aircraft to Chicago (I had to fly to Chicago first, then change planes for Indianapolis) was a wide-bodied McDonnell Douglas DC10. It was a beautiful aircraft, elegant and streamlined, but it was also half empty. I noticed this a lot on the flights I took within America; there were usually heaps of empty seats and yet they often had wide-bodied aircraft operating the route. Definitely a sign of those times. The flight to Chicago took three hours, and was very comfortable, as you can imagine, being half empty. As often happened when I was flying alone, businessmen came to talk to me and often bought me a drink. Mostly they just liked a chat with someone from another country. Sometimes they had other agendas, but I never felt threatened. An aircraft was somewhere I always felt supremely confident in and besides, at the end of the journey we had completely different commitments and went our separate ways.

Recently, I found an address book from that era and one of the blokes in question, called Jerry, had given me his work address and phone number as well as his home address and home number. He'd said to look him up if I was ever back in San Francisco. I wonder what would have happened if I had? An angry wife, maybe?

29

Indiana

What a contrast Indiana was from the dazzling Pacific coast. Certainly, the mid-west was pretty enough – everything was green and spring blossoms and flowers were blooming in gardens – but here it was the people I met who made a big impression. I warmed to them instantly and they to me.

I mentioned in an earlier chapter that Harold was my contact in Indianapolis. Just to jog your memory, I'd met him during a tour of Westminster Abbey. We'd chatted and exchanged addresses and my going to visit him was one of those 'seemed like a good idea at the time' situations. Now, however, I was beginning to feel a little uneasy. I know it sounds mean, but I thought he was really quite geeky (in today's language) and I wasn't remotely interested in him romantically, so what on earth was I doing there? It was too late to pull out.

It turned out that Harold must have had some misgivings of his own, as when we met at the Indianapolis airport we just shook hands and said 'Hi.' Phew. He'd organised for me to stay with his friends Bonnie and Gene in Lafayette. I remember first, though, being taken to his sister's house for dinner. She was lovely; very welcoming and kind. He then drove me to Bonnie and Gene's to stay for the week and I didn't ever see him again. He was certainly very…different. I was relieved, though, and Bonnie and Gene and I took to each other immediately and so began a wonderfully fun-filled week, one of the best on my American tour.

Bonnie and Gene were a thirty-something couple. Gene was tall, dark and good-looking and Bonnie was lively, funny and quite large, not that it mattered. I barely noticed. They had a son too from Gene's first marriage and he was a nice kid. He told his mates at school about the Australian air hostess who was staying at his house.

One day we were having a discussion about Australia, and the subject of native animals came up. Bonnie and her friend Pat were very taken with the cute and cuddly grey Qantases. It didn't take me long to work out that they meant koalas and they'd mistakenly thought the word was a Qantas bear because of a TV commercial running at the time for Qantas Airways, before Qantas flew domestically as well as internationally. I was able to set them straight on that one, although I thought it was cute that they called koalas Qantases.

That week in Lafayette was so enjoyable and very relaxing. We went out to breakfast, which was something Americans liked to do. It was a custom that took off later in Australia as well. Again I was taken aback by the serving sizes. For example, if you ordered an omelette, it came with lots of melted cheese and about four slices of toast, besides the toast already on the table; or if you chose pancakes there were stacks piled with blueberries and sour cream. Of course there was endless coffee and also jugs of water placed automatically on the table. In Australia. you only got water on request, although we caught on later. I'm not having a dig about food serving sizes, but at the time it was surprising. because Australia had smaller servings. We have now well and truly caught up. I also came to know about drive-through banks, mega-sized gas-guzzler cars that everyone seemed to be driving, takeaway doughnut outlets and shopping malls that seemed endless.

Gene played in a band and one night we all accompanied him to a gig at a venue called the Elks Club. A great night was had by all, lots of dancing, giggling and consumption of countless Harvey Wallbangers. I remember my mum commenting that I looked drunk in one of the photos taken that night. Well, yes Mum, that's because I was. I guess the best way to describe this gig was that it was something like a 60/40 dance in Australia. Dress was fairly casual, but you could dress up if you wished.

The American Airlines Boeing 727 that took me from Indianapolis to Chicago and on to Toronto.

I went to see *Towering Inferno*, the big-budget Hollywood disaster movie at the time. Pat, Bonnie's friend, and I went together. There were many edge-of-the-seat moments, which caused Pat to scream and grab hold of me, which in turn made me laugh at all the wrong moments.

I didn't want to leave Bonnie and Gene, but my schedule was fairly tightly planned and I was due to fly to Toronto. I wasn't at all sure now about visiting Ryan, who I'd met in New Zealand, but I still wanted to see what Toronto was like. Sadly, Bonnie and Gene and I said goodbyes at Indianapolis airport, with a vow that I would return the following year. Instead, I visited in 1977.

When I'd returned home, Gene sent a number of photos, as he was a keen photographer. He'd taken quite a few of me at their home and the airport, including several of my American Airlines Boeing 727 careering down the runway and out of sight.

30

Toronto

Toronto is, and was back in 1975, a very large and super-modern city. I got the impression, looking at its high-rise skyline and sheer size, that it was the most modern and progressive-looking city I'd been in so far. I'm sure Chicago could give it a run for its money, but I didn't spend any time there and was only really aware of its might when we climbed over the Sears Tower, all 1,450 feet of it, when sailing by in the aircraft en route to Toronto. That was quite a sight. The tower is a real landmark of Chicago. Built in 1973 as the Willis Tower, but now more commonly known as Sears Tower, it is 110 storeys high and for twenty-five years it was the tallest building in America, until it was surpassed by the new World Trade Centre in 2014.

My friend Ryan, who, as I've already mentioned, I met on my 1973 New Zealand tour, lived with his family just outside of Hamilton, Ontario, which seemed to be a pleasant leafy, garden suburb. I recall their big rambling old house, which was a bit like a Tardis. The house was two-storey and seemed huge, but no doubt it had to be to accommodate three boys growing up. Ryan had two brothers, all of whom were no doubt pretty boisterous. The garden was large and well cared for. The backyard sloped down to the shores of Lake Ontario; although maybe I can just remember seeing the lake. I'm not quite sure, as it's so long ago. Across the road were the Burlington Botanic Gardens, which were full of colourful spring flowers when I visited, helped along by some fairly warm, humid weather.

Although my six days there weren't as relaxed as in Indiana, the family was very good to me and I certainly saw plenty of interest. What made the stay just a bit awkward was that Ryan's mum seemed keen for us both to be together and she'd say, 'Ryan, sit here next to Lindsey,' or 'Ryan, why don't you take Lindsey here, there or wherever.' It seemed that she was telling Ryan what to do, instead of letting him decide for himself. I also felt that she saw me as potential daughter-in-law material. I could be wrong, but I don't think so. My vibe antenna was in overdrive and I always took notice of a gut feeling. Any holiday romance feelings had long since fizzled out, certainly for me. I couldn't read Ryan, so I'm not sure what he felt. Besides, I was pretty sure I wouldn't have wanted to marry someone overseas and I preferred to find a partner within Australia, so that all made me feel rather uncomfortable, though I'm quite sure that wasn't the intention.

When I arrived at the Toronto airport, Ryan took me straight to the family holiday house on the shores of a lovely lake ringed by forest. There seemed to be mostly large expanses of water and pine forests and later, when I was in Sweden, the scenery there reminded me of this particular region of Canada. Ryan told me that people went ice-skating on the lakes in winter. It was a long weekend in Canada and families were in their weekend homes or shacks and many of them were out on the lake when the four of us – Ryan, his mum, dad and me – took a ride over the lake in their motorboat before dinner. I was led to understand that there were bears in the forest; indeed, it looked like that kind of forest, a bit dark and scary, but I tried not to think too much about bears when I had to visit the out-house. At least there didn't seem to be any spiders as there would be in Aussie outdoor loos (often dubbed dunnies). You should check out a famous Aussie song, 'There Was a Redback on the Toilet Seat', by Slim Newton, an Aussie country music singer/composer. It's a humorous song. Many Aussie outback loos are often just like the one in the song; sometimes a snake manages to sneak in as well.

I also remember seeing an abandoned beaver dam across a creek or stream and marvelled at the hard work that beavers put into constructing them. I bought a couple of little ornamental beavers, which I think I gave to my mum.

Me at Niagara Falls, having just been on the Maid of the Mist ferry, which rakes tourists under the falls. The roar is deafening.

One day I went sailing in a canoe with Ryan. I bet his mum loved that. She insisted on my wearing a face cover to protect me from black flies; nasty biting little critters that enjoy the taste of foreign blood. I was the only person wearing one of these fashion statements, which caused much good-hearted amusement among others sailing on the lake. It must have looked insanely funny and I have a cringe-worthy photo to remember it by. I must say, though, that I enjoyed the canoe experience and I coped better than I'd imagined with using the oars to paddle. I was so glad we didn't fall in, which would have been humiliating, not to mention freezing cold.

Visiting Niagara Falls and sailing underneath was something I was glad not to miss. Of course we all had to wear raincoats, which I think were yellow with matching hats, so we all looked a bit like Paddington Bear, some more than others of course. I don't have a raincoat photo, but there is one of me taken afterwards looking like a drowned rat. The falls were certainly spectacular and the roar of the water was like nothing else I've ever heard before or since, except for maybe the geothermal power plant at Wairakei, which is part of the Taupo region volcanic zone, in New Zealand. I also saw the Welland Canal at St Catherines that day and clearly recall learning about that and the St Lawrence Seaway in social studies at school. I was excited too, to have been in New York State for just a couple of minutes. I can at least lay claim to having been there, even if not to NYC itself. One side of the falls is in Canada and the other is in the US.

Later in the week we went to the movies in Hamilton and saw *Shampoo* with Warren Beatty, Goldie Hawn, who I've always loved in movies, and Julie Christie. I saw that film again on TV last year and couldn't get over how young all the stars looked then. Yes, I know forty years makes a difference. I also realised how dated the movie was. I did enjoy it at the time, though, and I loved the 70s fashions too.

Next stop Vancouver. I breathed a sigh of relief, as I was ready to head back to the west coast to my friends Kathy and Leslie.

31

Back to the Wild, Wild West

Vancouver is not of course the wild, wild west. I was just having a bit of fun with the title of the well-known movie starring Will Smith. I'm sure parts of western Canada are very wild and no doubt beautiful and remote too, but I didn't see those areas.

I was glad to be back in Vancouver with my friends Kathy and Leslie. This time I stayed with Kathy and her lovely little daughter Jennifer, who was only five at the time. I wasn't really into small kids back then; however, Jennifer was a very appealing little girl.

We saw plenty of Leslie and Glen and one night we had a barbecue at their house. Leslie was a fantastic cook and produced an absolutely mouth-watering dessert of bananas that she sautéed in butter and rum which we polished off with ice cream. I remember eating outside and although it was now chilly, being the Pacific north-west, the coolness was welcome after the humidity of Toronto.

We also visited the Vancouver Zoo, and an American Indian restaurant, staffed by attractive young people who to me looked to be genuine American Indians. The food there was delicious, especially the salmon. I was intrigued generally by the American Indian influence in Vancouver, from the totem poles in parks and on the streets, to craft shops. I wish I'd bought some of the unique turquoise beads and pendants on display, but by now I was running low on money and traveller's cheques. This culture was completely new and unique to me. I wish I could remember more. However, I did buy an American Indian colouring-in book, which I still have. One day, I might just get busy and do some colouring; after all, it's very popular these days.

My favourite outing of all, was the day trip that Kathy and I took to Vancouver Island and its capital Victoria. There are so many reminders in western Canada of Queen Victoria. The Canadians loved her and she almost has superstar status. There's even Victoria Day, a public holiday in her honour. A ferry took us to the island, a journey of two to three hours. We ate breakfast on board: one of those colossal omelettes I've told you about. Then we ventured out on deck to get fresh air. There was plenty of that on offer and I have a photo of a very wind-blown me gazing out across the small gulf islands. I had the sensation of being much further out to sea than we actually were and of being thousands of miles from anywhere, which I really enjoyed. I was truly able to blow away some of the cobwebs from my more stressful week in Toronto.

In Victoria, I was surprised and delighted to see double-decker red buses like I'd seen in London the year before. Western Canada is certainly more influenced by England, whereas in Toronto and other eastern Canadian cities the emphasis is definitely French. Toronto is probably a mix of both.

Kathy and I went to the Empress Hotel for drinks and possibly a snack, although we weren't particularly hungry after that mega-breakfast. We sat in the Bengal Lounge. The interior was, as you might imagine, traditional English and very upmarket and elegant. I have an enlarged photo of the exterior of the hotel in my home. It's an imposing building – the word 'edifice' springs to mind – and covered in ivy. I'm glad it's still there and hasn't been replaced by something super-modern and brash. I imagine it would be pretty popular and expensive; an ideal honeymoon setting.

My last night was at the harbour-facing Sylvia Hotel, where, to my joy, there was a dance floor. We danced until the early hours of the morning while the harbour lights twinkled outside. I had to catch the flight at around seven a.m. The disco era was in full swing and some of the songs I remember from that night were 'Lady Marmalade' by La Belle, 'That's the Way I Like It' by K.C. and the Sunshine Band, 'When

Will I Be Loved' by Linda Ronstadt, 'How High the Moon' by Gloria Gaynor and another of hers – 'I Never Can Say Goodbye'. You might have guessed I liked Gloria Gaynor.

I did have to say goodbye, though, to Kathy, Leslie and Glen. I'd already said goodbye to little Jennifer and given her a present, and Vancouver, which of course was sad. I think I stumbled onto the aircraft for the long haul back across the seemingly endless Pacific Ocean at forty thousand feet. This time the aircraft was a McDonnell Douglas stretched DC8, which was similar in size and appearance to the Boeing 707. It was daylight the entire trip back, I think, whereas going over had seemed like a very long night. I still find it hard to wrap my head around the mysteries of the International Dateline, as was especially evident by my late arrival back to report for work. This was usually grounds for dismissal from the airlines. However, my supervisor at that time, who was lovely, understood how I'd come to miscalculate the dates by crossing the International Dateline and she gave me another chance, for which I am eternally grateful.

I decided that I was in love with America and Canada and the people. Two years later, I returned to see some of my friends there. They might be surprised to know how often I still think of them and our wonderful times together. I love each and every one of them for their genuine kindness and generosity. Maybe, if we'd had the internet back then, we might still be in touch. Who knows?

I have two beautiful black and white photos of the view from Grouse Mountain, a lookout point just out of Vancouver and another mountain scene. They were taken by Glen, who, as I may have mentioned, worked as a photographer for one of the Vancouver newspapers. These are really very special photos and a great reminder of the May of 1975.

32

'Uh, Oh, We're In Trouble'

The song title 'Uh Oh, We're in Trouble' for this chapter fits in with this true story perfectly. You'll see as you read on. Firstly a little bit about the song origins. It was composed by a British girl band Shampoo in the early 90s. Some of you may remember it. Apparently, the name Shampoo derives from the excuse the girls made when turning down dates – they had to wash their hair. I first became aware of the song when I saw the St Trinian's 2 movie in 2007. It was one of the songs on the soundtrack. I enjoyed the movie immensely and the music, as it's so lively, naughty and lots of fun. Another great song from it is 'We've Got the Beat', which you might like to look at later on YouTube. You'll want to get up and dance, I promise. I know I've digressed, but I'm sure you won't mind. Anyway, on with this story, which is a real doozy and my own personal favourite.

Around the early 80s (about 1981 or 1982), the powers-that-be, the management of ASA, decided that our little airline, fondly dubbed the Country Club, needed an image revamp. We had smart new uniforms, fortunately not too influenced by the more ghastly 80s fashions of the time. We had new logos for the planes too; a piping shrike, sort of like a magpie, and a special ceremony to give them names of iconic South Australians. For example, *The Douglas Mawson* (an Antarctic explorer); *The Daisy Bates* (a welfare worker among Aboriginal people and an anthropologist); and *The Sir Hans Heysen*: (a famous South Australian artist). We even had advertising on the telly and more upmarket catering. Tea, coffee, biscuits and bar service were still provided on shorter flights such as Whyalla or Port

Lincoln, but the lucky ones on longer flights got a proper dinner or breakfast, all dreamed up by a then-fashionable restaurateur in trendy North Adelaide. I can't remember the name of the restaurant; I think it specialised in French or Italian cuisine, or maybe some of both. If you had visited this fancy place, you probably would have been served nouvelle cuisine. Remember that awful trend for serving microscopic serves of food which usually tasted great but took about two seconds to eat?

Well, one morning, as we were preparing for an early flight, either Broken Hill or Mount Gambier, which both took around an hour and twenty minutes, my friend Di and I were checking off the catering. It was all too easy to leave stuff behind. On another occasion, someone took off with two tea urns, instead of one each of tea and coffee. Fortunately that was not one of my faux pas. Now, I don't remember whether we'd got a memo about what we were supposed to serve, or whether we didn't or just didn't see it, but we opened a drawer and in there were some frankly rather weird-looking, stripy quiche sort of things.

Di and I looked at each other and looked again at the weird quiche things. We opened the plastic casing of one and sniffed.

'Oh, that smells,' we squealed, wrinkling our noses. We opened another.

'Ooh, that smells too. These are really bad. Someone's left them there from last night and they've gone off. Those catering guys are so lazy.' It was always useful to blame someone else.

'These really need to go.'

Without further ado, we tipped the lot into the bin provided on the plane. Well, you would have too, if you'd seen and smelt them. We thought we'd done everyone a huge favour and avoided a possible botulism outbreak, and the possibility of the airline being sued, by chucking them all out.

Anyway, we thought no more about these offensive quiche things, until, back in the hostess lounge, after our tour of duty, our supervisor appeared.

'Hi, girls,' she beamed. How sad it was that her good mood wasn't going to last. 'How did the harlequin omelettes go? Did the passengers like them?'

Di and I stopped, looked at each other and then at our supervisor and said, 'Harlequin omelettes? What are they?'

'You know, girls, what you gave the passengers for breakfast this morning.' She was still smiling.

'Oh, those smelly stripy things we threw out,' one of us said. 'Were they harlequin omelettes?'

'You threw them out?' Our supervisor was no longer smiling.

'Yes,' we said cheerily. 'They looked green and smelled really bad. They were disgusting.' Talk about adding insult to injury.

Our supervisor now looked like a thundercloud. Believe me, our supervisor's black look was very black indeed and I'm surprised that she didn't generate her own lightning, like a volcano. We were standing there like stunned mullets, waiting for the cloud to burst. I must say I don't remember much of what happened after that. I'm surprised we still had jobs and I have no idea how the supervisor explained our misguided actions to the restaurateur, especially after our description of his debut offering of specially made and no doubt rather expensive omelettes. I do remember that most of the blame went to me, as we had a junior/senior system in place and the senior was always the older of the two and had to be in charge of everything. So it was her fault if things went wrong. Of course I had to write a report about what happened, but I have no memory of what I said in order to try to explain. I know the story did the rounds of the airport, which after all was a hotbed of gossip; it still is. I'm quite sure everyone laughed about us, as Di and I do now. These days I find it absolutely hysterical and it cracks me up every time.

33

In Praise of Ploughman's Lunches and Peter Rabbit

Food can often be a highlight of an overseas holiday, along with scenery, shopping and making new friends. Food is pretty memorable, hopefully only in a good way. I've been extremely fortunate not to have suffered from food poisoning on any of my travels, but I've heard of many a tale of woe. It must be awful to fall ill in a foreign country and be unsure as to where to go for the best, most effective treatment.

A friend of mine once did a tour of Europe and Turkey in the early 70s with Contiki. It was her turn to do the shopping and cooking in Istanbul, so she went to the butcher's shop with a friend. I'm not sure what they asked for, but he sold her a bag of entrails. I often wonder whether they actually cooked them and, if so, whether everyone was OK afterwards.

While writing this, I remembered that I did get some sort of bug in Bali (surprise, surprise). We'd taken a day trip up to the north coast of Bali (Singaraja) and hired a taxi. We stopped for lunch somewhere and admittedly I wasn't too impressed with the standard of hygiene, but also the taxi wasn't air conditioned, so of course it was hot and steamy, and the road very winding; not only that, but diesel fumes seemed to be seeping into the car. I was never sure whether my rather violent but short-lived bug was the result of food I ate or diesel fumes, which I must say made me feel really nauseated. However, my husband John wasn't sick. Anyway, sometimes it's hard to pinpoint exactly what might have caused it. How funny to think I'd forgotten about it until that moment.

Special, tasty food is often synonymous with a memorable setting or interesting location. Maybe fish and chips in an English pub; something delicious and exotic like Murtabak in a bustling Singapore market; perhaps fresh tropical fruits in an open-air restaurant on a colourful Bali beach; or a typically French casserole in sauce that only the French can create, consumed with relish in a little café overlooking a mediaeval town square. Then again, maybe a dish of Brussels mussels for dinner at a little bistro in the floodlit Grand Place in Brussels or some divinely creamy New Zealand ice cream for dessert; or maybe some pan-fried barramundi, eaten while gazing at the Pacific Ocean rolling in at Manly beach in Sydney.

I've been fortunate enough to lay claim to all of the above, but, do you know, the absolute winner hands down was simply bread and cheese: A good old ploughman's lunch. In November 1983, John and I were in the UK on a Britrail tour of England, Scotland and Wales. During one section of the journey we came to the Lakes District and stayed for about four days. One morning we took a long walk from our base at Windermere to Sawrey, home of Beatrix Potter. The day was fine and the heavy rain from the day before had abated. I remember it was a Sunday and a church bell rang through the valley, which sounded lovely. We walked past lakes, lanes and streams and even climbed over a stile. I'd always wanted to climb over a stile, ever since reading many English children's books in which the kids often hopped over a stile or two. Pretty often they'd find a nasty big snorting bull awaiting them in the field.

Needless to say, after all this, we were ravenously hungry and found refuge in a free house in Sawrey, where we both ordered a ploughman's lunch. We certainly had the appetite of ploughmen by then. Our orders came and consisted of the freshest home-baked breads and local farm cheeses we've ever had, before or since. Of course, we washed it down with some of the local ales and still had room for dessert. We made short work of apricot slices and farm cream and finished with beautifully hot coffee. I should explain here that a free house is a

John walking along a country road in the Lake District.

pub not owned or controlled by a particular brewery and therefore not restricted to one brand of beer or ale.

I've already said that the location can be as memorable as the meal, and across the road from the free house was a real, live, almost identical to the original, Mr McGregor's garden. There was even a scarecrow and lookalike Mr McGregor, though I'm sure that wasn't his name, pottering among his rows of vegetables. We almost expected to see Peter Rabbit wriggling through the fence in his little blue jacket and were a bit surprised and quite disappointed when he didn't materialise.

John and I have often talked about that day: the meal and the walks, both there and back. On our return trip, with the sun low over the autumn-leaf-draped Lake Windermere and the air growing chilly, we came upon an old lake house, which the locals told us was haunted. I must say it had a haunted look about it and was in a perfect location; solitary and secluded.

So the best meal ever, Mr McGregor's garden with an imaginary Peter Rabbit and a haunted house in one day is pretty unbeatable. What's your magic meal moment?

Some of you might wonder why we didn't visit Beatrix Potter's house. Being autumn and the off season, many homes and some museums weren't open to the public. We had to be content with peering over a beautiful old stone fence beside a fast-flowing stream.

34

New Zealand, My Narnia: South Island

I've left the best almost till last: New Zealand. I've been fortunate enough to have visited three times. After Australia, I think it's the most thrilling place on the planet. New Zealand is only three hours' flying time away from Australia if you're leaving from Sydney, Melbourne or Brisbane. Now South Australians can exit from Adelaide to Auckland, which takes four hours. Then add an extra hour or two if, after landing in Auckland, you need to fly to Christchurch or Queenstown to connect with a tour.

It all began, I think, in 1973. I was in my early twenties when I first set eyes on the snowy Southern Alps, stretched across the horizon like a giant wave. I was entranced, and also by the lush green countryside on the Canterbury Plains, dotted with sheep, before climbing into the Alps. Of course many a joke refers to New Zealand's sheep, but it wouldn't be quite the same without them. Even the air smelt different; crisp and fresh. In 2002, with my husband and children, I saw New Zealand through three other sets of awe-struck eyes and more recently, in 2011, I felt exactly the same. I'm madly in love with New Zealand and probably always will be.

I have no house there, yet it's my second home. It's my Utopia, my Nirvana, my Magical Mystery Tour and my Narnia. Thank you, C.S. Lewis, for letting me borrow your Narnia idea for a short while. I greatly admire the *Chronicles of Narnia*.

I wrote 'New Zealand, My Narnia' five years ago, following my most recent tour in August 2011, which was six months after their February 2011 earthquake.

This chapter is mostly about that particular tour, although I've decided to include some highlights of the 1973 and 2002 trips. Of course the 2002 and 2011 visits weren't connected with my flying days, but all were completely unique and hold their own in my memory. I just can't leave some of these experiences untold. If I can't include them in *Here, There and Everywhere*, where can I put them?

Although John and I began our tour in Christchurch, I've chosen to begin the story in Fiordland, so the destinations aren't in order, but I like to think that this won't affect my memoir-telling at all. Besides, why let orderliness get in the way of a good story?

The Narnia parallel came to me while on a tour of Fiordland, which is right down towards the most southern part of the South Island. We'd had to wake early on this particular day and the sun was just rising and turning the misty clouds around the mountains pink As we drove further into the Fiordland National Park, frost and ice gave way to thick snow and peaks of nine to ten thousand feet towered either side of the bus. It was a crystal-clear morning, very still and icy cold. I thought to myself, this is what Aslan's country must be like. Perhaps others would imagine Aslan's country quite differently. To me, though, Fiordland somehow captures the essence of what Aslan's country represents. Do you remember the constant winter in Narnia the first time the children set foot in there? The rest of New Zealand, for me anyway, represents Narnia.

Our driver stopped the coach to let us take a short walk through a beech forest. Everything was hushed, except for the sound of running water and bird calls. The forest was dense with tree ferns, from which sunlit water droplets hung. We all felt inclined to whisper, so as not to disturb the peace and quiet. Delicate spiderwebs glinted in the pale lemon sunlight. The air felt like ice. On our return to the bus we had our first glimpse of the appealing but mischievous kea parrot. Everyone laughed when the kea pecked one of the young French girls from our tour bus on the backside. Cheeky little bugger; he surely must have been a bloke. These parrots are also very inquisitive and there were two standing on the steps of our bus, just as if they were going to board. 'Can we come too?' they might have been saying.

This area is astoundingly beautiful, wild and remote. A leisurely cruise on Milford sound takes you past Mitre Peak, which towers fve thousand feet straight out of the water and as you sail along, dolphins usually play by the side of the boat. On my 1973 visit, I was booked to take a flight from Milford to Te Anau, where our group was staying, but the pilot was ill, so I missed out. I imagine that it would be a spectacular flight, soaring over the jagged mountain peaks.

Weather here is unpredictable; indeed, right through the Alpine areas of New Zealand, weather can change in minutes and there's an ever-present risk of avalanches. Along the road we passed several large heaps of snow that were the remains of an avalanche. I discovered that strong earthquakes (between 7 and 8 on the Richter scale) are quite common here too.

It was a real privilege to be in Fiordland, even if only for a short time. Thank goodness for cameras and memories.

Of course, there are many other parts of New Zealand to admire. For instance, the rolling, gentle green farmland around Dunedin. Likewise, the rather dramatic train ride from Dunedin through Taieri

Reflections on a lake near Milford Sound.

Gorge to Middlemarch, the cutting built out of mountain rock in the nineteenth century by men who had few tools and certainly none of the modern ones that are used today. This railway was built by sheer willpower.

The wild west coast beaches were covered in sculptured driftwood and dark volcanic sand, reflecting an entirely different mood from the east coast. Aoraki Mount Cook is always a sight to behold, whether standing out against a clear sky or shrouded in grey mists, with just its tent-shaped peak showing. I can also recall a long-ago memory of Aoraki Mount Cook bathed in moonlight one night as I gazed up at it from my bedroom window; angry black storm clouds swirled around its peak. The storm and howling winds that followed kept me awake for ages, but what an incredible, unforgettable sight it was and definitely the best room with a view I've ever had. The storm, however, put a stop to another scenic flight some of us had been intending to take. A light aircraft was to fly us up to the Tasman Glacier and land on it, but the continuous wild winds and fog made the trip impossible. A bus took us instead. Were my booked scenic flights always to be doomed to cancellation?

I love the serenity of nearby Lake Tekapo. I think this is maybe my favourite part of the South Island, because it still seems untouched, although on our 2011 trip I did notice a larger tourist presence. Still, it isn't yet like Queenstown, which I'll write about later. On our 2002 holiday, with the kids, we once stayed overnight in a lovely chalet on the shores of Lake Tekapo. Earlier in the afternoon, I'd sat for hours, just gazing at the pale blue and silver water of the lake, surrounded by snowy peaks. To me, they looked like giant icebergs floating in a mysterious sea. You have probably guessed correctly that I absolutely love Alpine scenery. My dream is to have a holiday home on the shores of this lake and can you blame me?

However, Christchurch is very special to me too. This was perhaps the most difficult part to write about, as I've always loved Christchurch, but after two earthquakes, it was of course no longer as I remembered it. The CBD had become a red zone, a no-go area fenced off to the general public. I was shocked to find this city rather like a ghost town, where only cold winds and dust blew through empty streets and hard-hat workers went about their clearing up, which was a mammoth task A lonely little pile of snow sat in the middle of a road from a fall the previous week. It looked incongruous, yet somehow symbolic of a city in ruin, although I knew Christchurch would be rebuilt. It has been; just not the same as before.

It made me feel very sad indeed, as I'd last seen Christchurch as a small, vibrant city, with people, spring flowers and rattling trams, and of course its wonderful old buildings. My husband and children and I once stayed for a few nights in the old treasury building. At the time, it was a rather upmarket boutique hotel and an extra-special experience included by our very savvy tour organiser. It stood opposite the cathedral, which was destroyed in the earthquake, along with many other stone churches; indeed, the stone buildings generally fared the worst.

My husband and I went for a walk one day. Almost every church built of stone was destroyed. On one, the steeple had fallen off completely and was placed next to the main body of the building. So sad and quite surreal. Yet close by is Hagley Park, which we saw blanketed with heavy snow. A week later, however, Hagley Park was on television and was filled with daffodils and spring blossoms, and seemed untouched by the earthquake.

The wonderful Antarctic Centre, next to the Christchurch airport is always worth visiting. We took our two children there in 2002, and the 2011 visit was even better. A theatrette in the complex was showing a documentary about the Antarctic and really made us feel as if we were right there, on board a ship among the snow, icebergs and heaving seas. One rather astonishing special effect was the sea spray that flew up over the ship's deck and out into the theatre and, yes, we did get a bit wet. Amazing, unexpected and great fun.

The other attraction is a room which mimics the weather at the

Antarctic. You can enter this room, dressed in special boots and coats, and experience a wind chill factor of -26 degrees Celsius. Then comes the storm, where the sky darkens ominously, and you're surrounded by snow and thunder. It seems so real. If any of you go, don't miss it. An all-terrain, amphibious Hagglund ride, a vehicle which is used to travel over rough terrain in the Antarctic, is also a must; we took the kids and ourselves on it in 2002. It gave a whole new meaning to bumpy ride. People with back problems are advised not to take the ride, but the delighted squeals of passengers on board tells you how popular it is. Kids love it.

In 2011, the people of Christchurch were as friendly and welcoming as ever and were delighted to see tourists returning. Ours was the first bus tour following their deadly earthquake. The people were quite happy to talk about their earthquake experiences and we chatted with a couple in a luggage shop and they told us of how they saw buildings across the road from their shop crumble before their eyes, which would have been terrifying. As we walked around the city and suburbs, we saw the liquefaction coming up from underground and lying in great grey puddles. Apparently, rebuilding cannot be carried out over areas of liquefaction. Seeing Christchurch after the February 2011 earthquake was quite a sobering experience, remembering that many people died – about two hundred, I believe. We also had a great deal of admiration for the positive attitude and resilience of the Christchurch residents, who vowed to rebuild their lives and their city.

I imagine many of you have heard of Queenstown in New Zealand. These days, it's a big tourist drawcard, well known for skiing, adventure sports, vineyards and wonderful views. It's on the shores of Lake Wakatipu and surrounded by high, rugged mountains. It's a breathtaking place. Also terribly cold in winter.

My first visit was in 1973 and the tourism industry was in its infancy. I do think that Queenstown had a certain off-the-beaten-track charm back then. There weren't any resort or boutique hotels, but I recall staying for two nights in O'Connell's Hotel: a two-storey, rambling Tardis of a place with gracious, yet not grand, service and big solid staircases. In the mornings, even before breakfast, the staff would bring every guest a pot of tea and biscuits to wake up with. How lovely was that? O'Connell's captivated me and when I hear of Queenstown I immediately imagine that lovely old-fashioned establishment in the wide main street. On our 2002 visit, I discovered that O'Connell's Hotel had become O'Connell's shopping mall with specialty shops. Certainly things don't stay the same forever.

The Queenstown of the twenty-first century was much more built-up; it now had an international airport, luxury resort hotels and shops, lots more people but still the same magnificent scenery. Tranquillity can always be found on the shores of the lake, where you can lose yourself gazing at the mountains, especially as the sun is going down, and listen to the water lapping at the lake edge, or the lonely sound of the SS *Earnslaw*, a tourist steamer boat, that sails to a sheep station across the lake. Now there were some different activities to enjoy and my family to explore them with. One that is always outstanding is the jet-boat ride along the Shotover River and through Skippers Canyon. This is a hairy ride, and everyone screams through the canyon because its narrow rock walls seem to close in. As the jet-boat accelerates to an incredible speed, your life flashes before your eyes; yes, really. If the driver made a slight mistake, it would indeed be all over. Likewise, the 360-degree turn, performed out in the middle of the river by the highly skilled driver, sets off another bout of screaming. My kids accused me of screaming the whole time. Well, that's all part of the experience. Screaming is compulsory. I may not be the most adventurous of people but the jet-boat ride through Skippers Canyon is a must-do each time. I almost can't imagine jet-boating anywhere else; it's very special. If you're extremely, terribly brave, and probably young, they have bungee-jumping, parasailing and snowboarding. I remember our daughter wanting to see the bungee-jumpers leap from the Kawarau Bridge, the most famous sight for this sport, because that was where Orlando Bloom, from the Lord of the Rings movies, did his jump.

While you should 'never say never', I find it quite easy to say never to bungee-jumping.

After Queenstown came the wild west coast, which has a real frontier atmosphere. From this side of the South Island, you get to see another aspect of Aoraki Mount Cook, and the ocean is the incredibly treacherous Tasman Sea. At Greymouth, our tour group of 2011 boarded the Transalpine train back to Christchurch, from where we would catch the train the next morning up to Nelson, a town on the Pacific coast. From there, we were to proceed to Picton to catch the ferry to Wellington, across Queen Charlotte Sound and Cook Strait. In Greymouth, our run of beautiful crystal-clear but cold days ran out. On the train, the snow started, just gently at first. We were delighted to be passing through the Southern Alps as fresh snow was falling. At dinner, in our hotel, it kept coming and didn't let up. We found ourselves in the middle of a once-in-sixty-year Antarctic storm and we were thrilled. Some of us stood outside the front door of the hotel to just watch it; the large white flakes caught the outside lights, so they appeared to be lit up. Airports around the South Island were rapidly closing and driving on the roads was becoming hazardous. This huge weather event pursued us for the next few days; yet somehow, we always managed to be one step ahead.

35

Sometimes It's Just the Little Things: At Home and Overseas

Here are a few more snippets from my flying days. Names have been changed where necessary.

During the tea/coffee/drinks service on board, there was always a risk that we'd get sprayed in the face when opening a can of fizzy soft drink. The same could happen with beer. Under pressure, the drink would gush out like a geyser. Fortunately, this didn't happen too often, but one day I was crewing an afternoon flight and I was to go out afterwards. Unfortunately, the time at which we finished wasn't going to allow me time to go home to shower and change, so I'd brought clothes and toiletries for a quick change in the hostess lounge afterwards. You can imagine that I wasn't too impressed when the can of beer I was opening squirted up, out, and just everywhere; on my face, hair and uniform. I smelt like a brewery, and my clothes and skin felt horribly sticky. I still had to fly the leg back to Adelaide. I'd never felt less like going out afterwards, but I had planned to go with my husband John, and my friend Di, who was my co-hostess on that fateful flight, and who'd found it very funny, along with her husband Barry. They were collecting us at Adelaide Airport, so there was very little I could do except grin and bear it, which I'm afraid to say I didn't manage very graciously. At least it wasn't a first date.

In about 1980 or '81, a young blonde actress called Bo Derek graced the big screen. She was a real pin-up girl and she starred in a movie called *Ten* with Dudley Moore. Some of you may have seen it.

Anyway, one day on a flight to Kangaroo Island we had a plane load of schoolkids, as we often did, about eleven or maybe twelve-year-olds. I'll always remember one young lad, as we were checking seat belts/seats upright and so on. He looked up and said to me, 'Gee, you're prettier than Bo Derek.' Wow, now I looked like Bo Derek as well as Kim Novak (see 'Leerers and Lechers'). It gave me quite a buzz, but I bet he grew up to be a little smoothie and a big flirt. They do start young sometimes.

In 1978, my good friend from Kansas City, Zelma – Zee – and I took a Eurail trip in Germany, Swizerland and Austria. It was wintertime and very cold, as you can imagine. We often sought warmth and an evening meal in one of the delightful German inns. One evening we were in Rothenburg, a real fairy tale sort of town on the Romantic Road and it was even more so because of the snow lending quite an ethereal atmosphere. Once in the inn, we struck up a conversation with some local lads, or rather they did with us. Their girlfriends weren't too impressed, I can tell you. During our chat, these lads started referring to Zelma and me as bad wives. They'd got it into their heads that we were on the loose, apart from our husbands, though neither of us was married then and we certainly weren't wearing rings. I think they may have thought we were out for a good time. Thank heavens for their girlfriends, who by then had had enough of their blokes chatting up foreign girls and they said their goodbyes. For sometime after that, Zee and I referred to each other in letters as bad wives. It became a standing joke between us.

One of the lovely things that happened out of the blue was when, during a walk through Hyde Park in London, John and I stopped a while to look around. All of a sudden a little squirrel, just like Basil Brush, scampered across the grass and hovered around my feet. He inspected the toe of my boot and then, satisfied, scampered off again. A really special moment.

Another special moment happened in Harlech Castle in north Wales. John and I visited one day and, it being nearly winter, were the only tourists inside the castle walls. I loved it when these ancient buildings were almost empty; so much more atmospheric. Anyway, John climbed one of the tower staircases to walk along the turrets, but I didn't fancy the idea, so I stayed and just enjoyed the peace and quiet and the feel of ghosts of centuries past. You could still see the outline of rooms and a huge stone fireplace, but best of all a robin redbreast flitted around just a short distance away. He/she stayed and kept me company until John came down from the lofty turrets. We still have a photo of the bright-eyed, pretty little robin.

In England, I loved cities surrounded by walls. John and I got a real kick out of taking a walk around the historic walls of Chester as there was a railing on both sides, unlike York, where there was one on one side only.

Our 1983 Britrail tour was longer than some of our other overseas jaunts. We were away for about five weeks and in that time consumed quite a bit of pub grub – that is, chips with everything. Of course we both put on weight, and had a bit of a wake-up call when one day we were met at Betwys-a-Coed railway station in North Wales by our B&B host. Suddenly, there was a loud ripping sound. It was the seat of John's pants splitting as he climbed into the car. Luckily it hadn't happened before that and at least we were headed to the B&B, where John could change. John, of course, was really embarrassed.

A little later on the same tour, we were travelling from Chester to Hereford. It was a very long day, with several train changes and long waits, stamping up and down on cold, draughty stations. Towards the late afternoon, we stopped at Worcester, where a whole lot of soccer fans boarded and we ended up squashed together with numerous others in the guard's van, which was certainly preferable to staying in the carriage with the unruly soccer lot. Anyway, by the time we arrived in Hereford and found our accommodation, we were insanely hungry. We went for a walk into the town and I think stopped at about the first likely place that was actually open for something, anything, to eat. It was a greasy spoon place, where fast, snacky type of food is served, like hamburgers, chips, hot dogs and bacon and egg sandwiches. The food was some of the best we'd had, though, and much tastier than you buy at many of the fast-food chains. We were extremely hungry, but our bacon/eggs/fried bread serves were tasty and well prepared. However, a glance behind the counter put us off somewhat, as the woman working there was sneezing near our food and told us, in her West Country accent, that she had a bad cold. We pretended we hadn't noticed and continued our meal with large slices of lemon meringue pie. Days later, we both came down with colds. Was that the justice for eating, and hugely enjoying, our lemon meringue pie?

Back to 1976. I met Zee on my tour of Scandinavia and we became firm friends. Towards the end of the tour, we were staying in a hotel in Denmark. I don't remember the name of the town, except that it was very quaint and I do recall seeing storks nests on local chimney tops and possibly even the odd stork thrown in for good measure. Also staying at this hotel was another tour group with a similar itinerary. Their tour guide was a real playboy type called Richard, an Austrian from Salzburg. His friend, presumably someone from the tour group, was a young, very good-looking Israeli who was at that time in the Israeli army. I think he may have come from Tel Aviv. Richard and this other bloke chased us around and around the revolving door of the hotel. Zee and I of course were giggling like idiots. Later, we went for drinks with these two. We both really liked the Israeli soldier, but not Richard, as he was a sleaze. He'd apparently been watching us, he said, throughout the tour when we happened to be at the same place. What a stalker.

During my flying days, the two main domestic airlines were Ansett Airlines of Australia (Airlines of South Australia was, as I've mentioned before, their subsidiary) and TAA or Trans Australia Airlines. At that time, both provided economy and first-class service. One of the nicest perks, besides the heavily discounted overseas airfares, was that whenever Ansett or Airlines of South Australia staff flew interstate, we usually got put into the first-class section of the cabin. I should explain here that we didn't receive a discount from TAA. If travelling on one of the early morning flights, you'd be served breakfast, and a full lunch around noon with free bar service and champagne. Dinner was served in the evenings, likewise with free bar. We all loved this benefit of course and would be quite put out if we didn't get upgraded. Spoilt little minxes. A few years later, Ansett and ASA crews were able to fly around Australia four times a year, completely free, and usually first-class besides. What a life.

It's just as well we had those perks, because there were some cabin crew who were not at all agreeable to fly with. One who comes to mind is Psycho Sandra. She was terribly moody, took offence at the least little thing and was sulky most of the time. On rare occasions, she could be quite pleasant, usually around men. You never knew which version you were going to get on the day. These days, you'd be right in wondering whether she was bipolar. We all hated flying with her and dreaded the idea of being rostered with her for a whole month. We were rostered into monthly blocks and had to bid for our choices. The more senior you were, the better the roster. Flying with a person like Sandra was sheer hell for a day, let alone a month. I think you can imagine that being more or less locked into the aircraft for several hours in close proximity with this psycho lady was hellish. Luckily for me, I didn't have to put up with her too often. Many people have the idea that cabin crew are all pleasant, even-tempered and with no hang-ups. Well, 'It ain't necessarily so.' Moodiness and antagonism is even harder to deal with in-flight than on the ground.

I once boarded an Ansett flight to Sydney, and as I was taking my seat, I became aware that the two hostesses standing nearby were having a rather catty argument. If I could hear it, no doubt other passengers could too. In that enclosed space, it created a tense and unpleasant atmosphere; not to mention the two concerned appearing unprofessional.

When we were in London, we went to the Victoria Palace Theatre to see a pantomime: *Dick Whittington and His Cat*. This was pantomime on a grand scale, such as I hadn't seen since I was a small child in Adelaide. It was an all singing, all-dancing extravaganza with well-known comedy stars of the early 80s. One of them was Clive Dunn from *Dad's Army*. Of course one of his oft-repeated lines on TV was 'Don't panic!' He had the audience enthusiastically yelling out, 'Don't panic, don't panic.' It was the best fun ever, so I was not at all impressed when John nudged me and reminded me we had to collect some photos, as we were headed off to Germany the next day. We had to leave the theatre twenty minutes before the end or the photo place would have been closed. I was very grumpy for the rest of the day. This was certainly a sign of the times. Today the photos would be safely saved on a mobile phone. Such was life back then.

In Salzburg, bedsides taking the *Sound of Music* tour, or visiting Mozart's house and his museum, or going to some of the many wonderful theatres on offer, there is another short tour that shouldn't be missed. These are the Salzburg catacombs, originally believed to have been a secret place for early Christians to meet and pray. Until Constantine became Emperor of Rome in the fourth century AD, it was extremely perilous to be a Christian, and often punishable by death. Entering this ancient, hallowed space was a sobering experience. We both felt awed at being in an environment in which the early Christians had worshipped, and we wondered at their incredible courage. The appearance of the catacombs is hard to recall; they were certainly dim and unadorned, though I think there may have been some frescoes or murals on the walls. However, there was an overwhelming sense of peace and serenity, only broken by the guide in her gently Austrian-accented English. When we re-emerged into daylight, we learned that the Salzburg catacombs are hewn out of the Monchsberg, which is a mountain named after Benedictine monks. If we were ever fortunate enough to be able to return to Salzburg, the catacombs would definitely be at the top of the 'must visit' list.

One morning, towards the end of our 1983 Britrail tour, we awoke fully expecting to spend about another week in London. By the end of the afternoon, we had to pack our cases within about half an hour, with a taxi waiting outside our B&B to rush us to Heathrow for a Singapore Airlines flight leaving for Australia about seven-thirty p.m. Why did this happen? Did we make the flight on time and what significant event took place after we'd left London? These questions and more deserve a later chapter all of their own.

36

New Zealand, My Narnia: North Island

The spectacular Antarctic snowstorm followed us from Christchurch, all the way up the Pacific coast in the train, up to Nelson and across Cook Strait to Wellington and the lower North Island, just stopping short of Rotorua. Of course all the people on the bus tour found it incredibly exciting and, fortunately for us, it did not halt our progress. We seemed always to be one day ahead of the worst, most disruptive aspects of this 'perfect snowstorm', as the press called it. Others weren't so lucky. The storm resulted in cancellation of flights in and out of Queenstown, where we had been only days before enjoying perfect sunny winter weather. Dunedin and Christchurch were also affected, as well as Wellington. Roads and schools were closed; power blackouts were reported, besides further damage done to earthquake-affected buildings. Work in the red zone at Christchurch had to be abandoned for a while because of increased hazards due to the snowy conditions.

On our last evening in Christchurch at dinner, the hotel dining room was almost packed to the ceiling and quite chaotic, with people whose flights had been cancelled and who were seeking accommodation and a hot meal. The staff managed brilliantly, though, and delivered delicious meals to many stressed, upset customers.

I'll always remember one young couple, from Auckland, the northern city, who'd managed to fly as far as Christchurch. They had aimed to fly to Queenstown for the weekend, but their plans had been turned upside down. The weather conditions prevailed for several days. They were trying to be positive and upbeat, but our hearts went out to them. I'd like to think that at some time, they had their weekend and enjoyed a rip-roaring time.

The next morning, our group awoke early to be driven to Christchurch railway station for the trip to Nelson. I recall looking out from our bedroom window just before leaving. Our room was next to the outdoor patio and pool area and absolutely everything was covered in snow and looked quite incongruous. Snow continued to fall as we boarded the bus and drove slowly through the icy, slippery, dark streets to the train. This was the first Coastal Pacific service since the February earthquake. Had it been the next morning, we wouldn't have been able to go, as the snowfalls had disrupted all travel, including trains.

Before I move on to our journey north, I want to tell you of an unfortunate, unpleasant incident. We'd needed to wake very early, as I've already said. The hotel staff kindly agreed to provide a light breakfast for us before leaving. This was at four-thirty a.m. and most of us were very appreciative of this, except for one loudmouth – there often is just one fly in the ointment.

Justine (not her real name) stood up, berating the hotel staff for not providing a cooked breakfast; she made sure that the rest of the people in the dining room could hear her rant. 'We pay for our breakfast,' she said petulantly and angrily.

The rest of our tour group were so embarrassed that we looked down at our plates, exchanging horrified glances. We just couldn't believe she was complaining. We were all so grateful to be given cereal, toast, and tea or coffee, by staff who had risen extra early just for us. Not only that, but the previous evening they had done a mighty job catering for the extra crowds of customers whose travel plans had been ruined. We felt as if she tainted the whole tour group. Following her outburst, we were all served with bacon and eggs, which by now nobody really wanted. However, we made sure that we thanked the staff effusively and told them what a magnificent job they'd done. We were glad to climb aboard our bus for the trip to the station. After that, no one thought very highly of Justine, who was wealthy, spoilt, self-centred and greedy.

The train journey itself was like something out of a documentary I once saw about Siberia. It was also very similar to what John and I had experienced in Austria and Switzerland back in 1981 (see 'The Case of the Lost Coats in the Sacks of Potatoes'). All the while, fresh snow was falling and it was impossible not to be enchanted by it. On the Pacific coast, as far up as Kaikoura, a range of mountains on one side of the railway line are usually snow-capped; but even on the opposite side, the snow was even seen on the beaches right down to the water's edge, and seals on rocky outcrops lay among snow. I often wondered how it felt for them. They didn't appear to be agitated, so maybe they had experienced such conditions before. It was just incredible. I know I've taken up quite a bit of time talking about the Antarctic snowstorm, but I'd never experienced anything quite like it. Even in New Zealand in July 1973, there seemed to be very little snow, at least on the ground. The event made a huge impression on my husband John and me, and, I think, the rest of our tour group. We were all quite captivated.

I must just briefly mention our day/night in Nelson in the northern part of the South Island and in the beautiful Marlborough wine-producing area. Here too, the wicked and icy wind was whipping through the streets, but the local people said that they didn't think they'd get any snow. 'It never snows in Nelson,' they told us.

That afternoon we were taken on a tour of one of the wineries, Brancott Estate and, as we were enjoying our tasting, we looked out the window and, lo and behold, the snow was falling in heavy thick flakes. We'll never forget this wine tasting and a snowfall in combo. It doesn't get much better than that; so you see you should 'never say never' – you don't know what's going to happen.

The ferry crossing from Picton to Wellington was very choppy and more than one person on aboard suffered the unpleasant symptoms of seasickness. Not us: we both have cast-iron stomachs, I think. Once more, we were fortunate to have crossed on that day, as the next day was even wilder and the ferry was cancelled. See what I mean about being just one step ahead of the weather.

In Wellington, after checking into the tour hotel, we decided to take refuge in the huge Te Papa Museum there. We had to brave crossing a couple of icy streets in blinding sleet and couldn't seem to find a pedestrian crossing. How we didn't get run over or slip under a car, I'll never know.

The Te Papa Museum is one of my favourite places in the North Island and my absolute go-to exhibit is the Awesome Forces, which focuses on the seismic and volcanic activity throughout the North Island, which is very active. There is a building here like a small house and bench seats are placed along each wall. You go in and sit down and wait for someone to press a button that sets off the simulated earthquake, 6.3 on the Richter scale, which was the intensity of the deadly earthquake in Christchurch in 2011. It's really unnerving, but I quite enjoyed feeling what this would be like, not least because of course we were able to walk out in one piece afterwards. Awesome Forces is a prelude to the real thing in Rotorua with its plopping mud pools and steam vents all over town.

Back we went across the slippery roads in still-falling sleet. The next morning we left Windy Wellington, which is its nickname, and its lovely harbour and drove northwards up the west coast, where there was more heavy snow. I remember one of the routes to take us to Rotorua was closed due to the snow and we took an alternative road, which I'd never been on before. There too, the countryside was covered by a white blanket. Our bus load of tourists was still delighted by the turn in the weather, as of course it hadn't inconvenienced us but just added romance, drama and gorgeous scenery. It was terribly cold, though!

Next came the three still-active volcanoes, Ruaphehu, Tongariro and Ngauruhoe (pronounced something like Narru-hoe-y). Not one of them was fully visible, as all were concealed by fog. To see the three of them together on a clear day is spectacular. I've only ever seen them like that on one occasion, back in 1973. It was an unforgettable sight. My tour group had just had lunch in the elegant Chateau Tongariro and when we emerged, there they were, three massive snow-capped volcanoes, standing benignly in the sun, gently puffing smoke. I do love volcanoes, especially from some distance away, yet close enough to admire.

There's another reason that this area is rather special to me as, back in our 2002 visit, the first of the *Lord of the Rings* movies had been released and our two kids were right into it. One afternoon, after a pie-in-a-paper-bag lunch in the Chateau Tongariro car park – such a contrast from lunch in the chateau itself twenty-nine years before – we drove further up the road on the slopes of Mount Ruapehu, which had been used, I think, as the setting for Mount Doom in the movie. Snow was falling rapidly and the park rangers were fitting all cars with chains. Our two kids had brought their newly acquired green Hobbit capes and we have a photo of them standing in falling snow which almost developed into a blizzard. Later on, the snow eased and we were able to go for a short walk on the slopes of the mountain and came across a little wooden bridge with a tumbling stream. It was such a pretty, hushed scene, as is often the case in a snowy landscape. Very memorable too, because the kids got soaking wet shoes and socks and came down with heavy colds and had to be taken to a doctor in Christchurch. No proper shoes for the weather, but they made sure they had their Hobbit capes.

Just before I head back to 2011, I simply must tell you about our stroke of luck in the North Island town of Mata Mata, back in 2002. Our daughter Joanna, who was fifteen at the time, had really done her homework about all things *Lord of the Rings* and had discovered that near the town of Mata Mata was the location of Hobbiton. She and our son Peter, then nine, were determined to see it so, after quite a few enquiries in local shops, we located a farm. My husband braved the farmer's rather aggressive dog to ask the farmer if he knew where to find Hobbiton. He told us that, yes, the Hobbiton set was still intact on his land and that, yes, we could go and see it. All he asked was that we shut the wooden gate of the relevant paddock so as the sheep wouldn't escape. So that's what we did. It was thrilling to see the little, almost cave-like houses set into the grassy hillsides. We walked over the wooden bridge where Gandalf and Frodo had crossed with the villagers, and saw the beautiful tall tree which I remembered so well from the movie. The kids were beside themselves and of course we have photos of them standing proudly in front of the cottages. Talk about getting in by the back door. Today, I imagine the site is crawling with tourists, who've all paid a premium for their tour, not that I blame them. I looked online and the cheapest day tour I could see cost $170. We now appreciate our self-guided tour even more, where the only sounds came from our kids, some sheep and the wind whispering through the Hobbiton trees. A very special day indeed.

Back now to 2011. I'm just crazy about Rotorua. I love the way steam rises from random vents throughout the city and countryside and the dark mud pools that plop and gurgle in their parks. I've even seen water boiling in drains. You could make a cup of tea or maybe even fry an egg, which could be fun to try. I love the slightly uncertain sensation that you could explode at any minute. I'll always remember the lady at our Rotorua motel telling us, 'One day we'll probably all just go boom.'

In 2002, our accommodation was in a motel right next to the Whakapapa Maori centre in Rotorua. In NZ, the 'wh' sound is pronounced as an 'F', so you'd better be careful how you say Whaka, lest it be misconstrued. This park boasts the Pohutu Geyser, which spouts boiling steam every couple of minutes. From our motel lounge room window, we could watch the geyser and it became quite hypnotic. There are also hot smooth rocks next to the geyser and they are lovely to sit on or lean against; very soothing for any sore spots. It's surprising how much noise the fumeroles make; the fizzing and hissing rises to a crescendo and at times it's hard to hear. The smell of sulphur permeates the entire town. The park also has a Maori crafts centre, where all sorts of beautifully made artefacts are for sale. I always wanted a straw basket and still regret not buying one.

One of the highlights of the 2011 stay in Rotorua was the seaplane.

The three of us; – John, Andrea, one of our fellow tourists, and I – all took off on Lake Rotorua and soared over forests and old volcanic craters. The flight was really something. Like that song by the Who, we could 'see for miles and miles' and as far away as White Island, a still active and quite dangerous volcano sitting in the Bay of Plenty. We were able to see the massive cracks and craters made by a spectacular 1886 eruption of Mount Tarawera in the Rotorua area. It was as if a very large zipper had ripped through one end to the other. History tells us that it destroyed the Pink and White Terraces, then regarded as one of the Seven Wonders of the World, and many people were killed. The strange and rather eerie thing was that eleven days before the eruption, tourists had sighted a phantom Maori war canoe on the shores of the nearby lake and noticed surging water levels. Apparently people had not realised that Tarawera was active. They soon found out.

I'd also love to tell you about Huka Falls, the jade-green gushing Waikato River, the geothermal centre and the thunderous hiss of the geothermal power station, but they will have to wait for another day.

The Bay of Islands, in the very north of the North Island, was new to both of us. The Narnia comparison cropped up again, when we were taken on a cruise to 'the Hole in the Rock.' I felt that I had found my way onto *The Voyage of the Dawn Treader*. I almost expected Reepicheep, the mouse, to show up on deck, wielding his sword. He wasn't there, but I watched dolphins play in some of the clearest turquoise waters I've ever seen. So this too may be Aslan's country.

I must say that the Bay of Islands gave us a chance to warm up and was quite welcome as of course until then we'd been really terribly cold. This part of New Zealand is famous for its magnificent kauri trees, and I hadn't seen anything quite as tall since the visit to Muir Woods in San Francisco. I managed to drop our camera here and John and I had quite an argument about it, as I think we were a bit tired and cranky by then. Fortunately, being a digital camera, the chip that saves the photos was OK but not the camera. We had to use the non-digital one, which luckily for us we had brought along as well.

Suddenly, it seemed, we were back in Auckland. I really like Auckland, as it reminds me quite a lot of Sydney. It has a large harbour and you can take ferry rides to various parts of the city. Auckland is also built on volcanic land, so there too it's possible to experience seismic activity, though I think not as much as Rotorua or Wellington. It's also not as big a city as Sydney, but the hills are much steeper. We got lots of exercise walking between the harbour and our hotel. The Auckland Tower is worth taking a rocket-like ride to the top for the view. John and I thought we were very brave as we walked over a glass panel through which you can see right down to ground level. I think they have something similar in Japan and probably other tall towers around the world. It was also great fun going to Denny's Diner, from where you could watch crazy people abseiling down the face of the tower. There's nothing so comfortable and 'smug-making' as enjoying dinner while watching others risk life and limb through their own choice. It provides great entertainment.

Finally came the morning of our return home, which we did, not in a train or through a wall, as in Narnia, but via the door of an Air New Zealand 767. I had booked us into business class as a special surprise for John and a once-off treat for us both. I was so glad I did, as there was an enormous amount of legroom, extra attention and champagne – yes, at breakfast. I felt like Patsy and Eddy from *Ab Fab*. There was enough food to make us groan by the time we disembarked. Definitely the way to end our Narnia-like holiday.

Then, there we were, dazed and a bit dishevelled, blinking in the bright artificial light of the real world, in Kingsford Smith Airport in Sydney, wondering whether one day we'd hear another call to return to our second home: to New Zealand, our hazy, dreamy island in the Pacific Ocean, so close and yet so far; our Narnia.

37

Now for Something Completely Out of Sequence, Part 1

The year 1976 was a memorable one for British people, as it was the year they suffered a severe heatwave. It was was the hottest year on record in England and in a single day four hundred people were treated for heat-related conditions. Big Ben even broke down for the first and only time in its existence.

In July 1976, I was passing through London again, en route to Scandinavia and northern Germany There had been a delay of a day, because, due to heavily booked aircraft, I and some other airline staff, who of course were always on stand-by, were offloaded even before we had a chance to board. Fortunately this didn't hinder my connecting with my tour, and another hostess from ASA had also been unlucky in securing a seat on that day's flight to London; so we teamed up and decided to share the expense of a room overnight in the nearby Tullamarine (Melbourne Airport) Travelodge Hotel.

Naturally it was a bit disappointing not being aboard the London flight, but Ellen and I made up for it with a drink or two in the Zodiac Bar, a dimly lit lounge with constellations glowing on the ceiling, then going to our room, where we ordered a plate of sandwiches from room service and raided the minibar. We sat in bed eating our sandwiches and watching the *Donny and Marie* (Osmond) *Show* on telly. Ellen had a great sense of humour and so we had lots of laughs. Ironically, that night they were performing a send-up of pre-flight demos and we both nearly fell out of bed laughing.

Early morning arrivals at Heathrow.

Next day, we were successful in boarding the British Airways marathon flight to London. Disembarking there in the early morning, I was surprised to find the temperature more like the heat at the beginning of summer day in Oz; so unlike the drizzly cold weather I'd experienced back in 1974.

There were three days to fill before I set out for northern Europe. Ellen was heading south to Greece and so we agreed to meet up and see some sights. We went to the Tower of London, Madame Tussaud's Waxworks and the Planetarium, which was blissful because it was a place to sit under cover, away from the heat of the day. We had to queue for everything in long lines of hot, irritable people and there were always bunfights for taxis. Anyone who's been to England or Europe in the summer months will know all about crowds. That's the reason I'll always prefer the autumn/winter months for Euro travel and of course many of my stories are set in those seasons. London buildings are also not geared to deal with high temperatures. There seems to be little or no air conditioning; all the effort goes into keeping homes and shops warm in the cold winters.

I may have told you that Ellen had a ribald sense of humour. Standing in Oxford Street, in the roasting sun, she swore at and gave the finger to any taxi drivers who didn't stop, but she did it in such

Tower of London.

a way that you couldn't help but laugh and on a few occasions I was nearly bent double, she was so hilarious.

The three days came to an end and I headed off to Victoria Railway Station to find my Scandinavian Highlights tour group, while Ellen flew off to Greece. She didn't have any accommodation booked and told me she'd sleep on the beach if necessary. That's just who she was: spontaneous and carefree in a way I wouldn't have dared. I'd have been the one to meet the axe-murderer. Ellen would have given him a sharp kick to the groin and gone on her way.

The train to Dover was crowded and stifling, with not a spare seat in sight, but I spent time getting to know two of my fellow-travellers-to-be, Chrissie and Zelma, who became long-time friends. At last we tumbled off the train and boarded the ferry to Ostend, where at least there was a chance to sit down and buy a cool drink, even if the windows were so grimy you could barely see out of them. However, I do recall standing on the deck, watching Dover Castle atop the dazzling white cliffs disappearing into the distance.

38

Now For Something Completely Out of Sequence, Part 2

The coastal city of Ostend in Belgium, for anyone who has ever been there, especially in summer, is an absolute hive of activity, jam-packed with incoming or outgoing ferries, huge tour buses, tour guides holding up placards to beckon the next lot of straggling tourists and many hotels. I imagine it's even busier now than it was back in 1976. Of course it is the largest coastal city in Belgium and I bet it's also a Mecca for pickpockets. However, that didn't happen this time; that would be further down the track in 1983 (see Robbed in Brussels).

Zee, Chrissie and I trudged wearily down the gangplank onto the wharf and finally found our Globus tour group. We were on our way at last, towards Holland, northern Germany, Denmark, Sweden and Norway, home of fairy tales, the midnight sun, trolls, Vikings and, best of all, Abba.

After a few hours, the bus pulled into a rest stop. I don't recall where it was, but it had some of the stinkiest, foulest toilets I'd ever seen and, what's more, you had to pay to use them. A very large, stern-looking woman barred the way, just in case anyone tried to avoid paying.

It's always fascinating meeting the fellow travellers on the bus. I find I can quickly sum up who I like, who I don't like and who should be avoided at all costs. We had quite a collection of characters on this trip. Our tour leader was Gerald; he was suave, immaculately groomed, well-spoken and more than a little pompous. He didn't appear to have much of a sense of humour, but he did have a good knowledge of the countries through which we travelled. The driver was a young, fair-haired Dutch bloke called Jan, I think.

There was an elderly Canadian man and his wife from Quebec. The husband had cancer and looked terrible; at death's door. Everyone wondered how on earth he'd even survived the flight across the Pond (you know, the Atlantic). This was to be his last overseas trip.

Another couple who I remember quite well were also Aussies and ran a motel in Tocumwal in country New South Wales. They were friendly and amiable, although the man, Brenton, seemed to enjoy tagging along with Zelma and me. I reckon he thought he was cool, hanging out with the young ones. He was, however, quite sexist and later in the tour often commented on what Zee and I were eating.

He'd say, 'If you eat too much of that, luv, you'll have a backside the size of a barn.'

I don't know why he included Zee, as she was very slim; I was more curvaceous – not fat, though. Another sign of the times, blokes commenting on what you were eating or what you looked like. Brenton seemed to delight in reminding me that, as an air hostess, I should be watching my weight. Anyway, his wife didn't seen to mind him spending time with us, so maybe she needed a break. Still, enough was enough and mostly we tried to avoid him.

I wish I could remember more of that tour. I loved it and had a great time. One event that's quite clear in my memory was the first evening stop, which was Zeeland in Holland. It being a lovely balmy summer evening, Zee, Chrissie and I went for a walk. At one stage, I was talking and not concentrating and very nearly walked into a tram coming around the corner. The tram driver yelled at me, which was understandable; after all, I probably gave the poor bloke a heart attack. Anyway, Zee and Chrissie pulled me back just in time. Phew! That was a close one, though.

Next day, we were headed to Germany and sped along the autobahn, past quaint towns with their church spires and stork's nests on chimney tops, and little red farmhouses. It was there that Gerald began to tell us about the adult nightclubs of Hamburg, where there is also a famous red light district. Apparently, there was an optional tour for those who were interested. He went on to say that the clubs were certainly not for the prim or faint-hearted. I'm not quite sure how exactly he described them (dark and seedy goes without saying), but it aroused our curiosity.

Zee nudged me and whispered, 'Ask Gerald to explain in more detail.'

'OK,' I whispered back, and so I did. To this day, I can't quite believe that I actually piped up loudly, 'What do they actually do in these clubs?'

I heard ripples of laughter from the people sitting behind us.

Gerald looked disdainfully down on us and said scathingly, as if addressing two wayward schoolgirls, 'Well, I think if you have to ask, maybe you shouldn't go.' He then turned his back on us.

We hadn't wanted to go anyway. We burst out giggling and made other plans.

After dinner, we boarded the bus again to go for a short night tour of Hamburg which included the harbour, the red light district, which I found boring and rather sad, and best of all a fountain which changed colours accompanied by music of Handel. Much better than going to a nasty, sleazy club.

39

All Roads Lead to Stockholm

Following the night in Hamburg, our Globus tour group was ferried across to Denmark. The ferry was very different from the rather grimy one that took us to Ostend. I enjoyed standing on the deck, inhaling the fresh air of a perfect northern Europe summer's day. It wasn't as hot as it had been in London, but a lovely twenty-five degrees, which reminded me of Tasmanian summer weather.

I must say that I can't recall how long the trip took or the name of the port where we rejoined the bus, but Denmark seemed to me to be so pretty. The fine summer weather showed the little villages with their red farmhouses and multicoloured flower boxes to perfection. We passed through green, gently rolling countryside to Copenhagen. We visited Amalienborg Palace with its green copper roof: I find those green roofs very attractive and they suit the style of buildings here. This is the home of the Danish royal family, but they didn't invite us in for lunch, spoilsports. We saw the Little Mermaid statue and took a tour of the Carlsberg Brewery, with a refreshing sample taste thrown in at the end.

The clearest memory I have of Copenhagen was Tivoli Gardens, a summer funfair park, as well as the hotel in which we stayed for two nights being extremely noisy, as it was on a main thoroughfare. I had the impression that Copenhagen was a city that never went to sleep. The hotel was the setting of another embarrassing incident, which I am compelled to tell you about.

I had no idea that the young driver on the bus, Jan, had developed a crush on me. The first time I became aware of it, I was standing outside our hotel after dinner. Zee, Chrissie and I were discussing where we might go for a walk, when along came Jan and also Brenton and his wife.

Chrissie said to Jan, 'My, you're looking very sharp this evening. Have you got plans?'

'Yes,' he replied, 'I'm going out with Linda.'

He kept calling me Linda, as he couldn't seem to understand Lindsey, which was OK. I didn't really mind.

Everyone turned to look at me expectantly. I felt pretty cross that he'd assumed that, just because he dressed up and asked me out in front of a group of people, I'd smile prettily and agree.

I was going to dig my feminist heels in and so I said, 'No, we're not. Jan hasn't asked me before now, so we're not going anywhere. Besides, I'm going to wash my hair.' Yeah, I know, the oldest date-refusing put-down in the book.

I felt a bit awful, because Jan looked both hurt and annoyed and I could tell he wasn't prepared for my reaction but I didn't care. Anyone who asked me out had to do it properly, so Zee and I turned up the street and started out on our walk, with the group gawping after us. I had to take a few deep breaths to get rid of my huff.

The next night we went to Tivoli, which I suspect was where Jan was planning to take me the evening before. Zee and I paired up and we had a whale of a time. We rode on a ferris wheel, got followed by some young Spanish blokes, ate fairy floss (cotton candy for you Americans) and even watched a classical ballet. To my surprise, Zee had never seen classical ballet performed before and she loved it; me too, being a ballet fan from since I was a kid. We had coffee and cake in a café where the décor was all pink and white; which topped off another perfect summer night.

Before leaving Copenhagen the next morning, I, for some reason, looked under my bed. I suppose I was just checking that I hadn't left anything behind. I hadn't but I did find a pretty scarf, which had come from Switzerland and which I have to this very day. I also found a coin, a krone with a hole in the middle. I took it back to Oz with me, where I had it made into a really attractive and original pendant. I still have that too. (Travel tip: make absolutely sure you inspect under your bed wherever you're staying. You never know what you might discover. Another time I found some English pounds; not enough to report to management, but enough to buy a glass of wine or coffee and cake. I mean, what else would you do with it?)

Jan was sulking and didn't speak to me for a few days. A bit later he tried again, but the next time I think he got the message. I wasn't going to be anything other than pleasant and polite. And firm of course.

Much as I'd enjoyed Denmark, I was really hanging out for Sweden, as it was the home of Abba, my idols. I think we took another ferry trip to Gothenburg and then there we were in Sweden. I was enchanted by all the beautiful lakes. At one of the Ramada inns we overnighted in, which I think was near Husqvarna, home of the famous sewing machines, the pristine Scandinavian room that Zee and I shared had a huge window overlooking Lake Vattern. Funny some of the things you remember, but not others. It was so relaxing, sitting in the comfortable chairs, just gazing through a forest of birch trees at the water; picking at peanuts and drinking beer from the minibar before dinner; and admiring the pale polished floors and deep cosy beds.

Of course at twenty-five, you don't want to sit still gazing at scenery for too long and once I arrived in Stockholm, there were other things to distract me: all the attractive blonde people with their gorgeous accents for one. I'm sure my neck was constantly swivelling.

One afternoon we were taken out to cruise on the large lake that is the main body of water in Stockholm, Lake Malaren. I was constantly blown away by all the water around Stockholm. Coming from Adelaide, which is one of the driest cities of Australia, I'd never seen so much in one place before, except for our coastal beaches, but not lakes. Once again, the weather was kind and I sat out on deck, dreamily watching the other boats on the water, the glinting green copper roofs of the gorgeous old buildings and wondering if, maybe, one of the houses hiding among the wooded areas on the shore happened to be the summer home of Abba. I must have thought I'd be lucky enough to just run into them randomly, but of course it never happened. Merely wishful thinking.

The old town of Stockholm was delightful too and it would have been fun to have spent more time there, exploring shops, cafés and the colourful flower markets. However, the icing on the cake for me was going to a disco in Stockholm. Zee and Chrissie and I must have asked someone at our hotel where to go and how to get there. It meant a short ride on their underground, one of the cleanest and nicest I've ever been in. The disco was upstairs in a large dimly lit room (somewhere in the city) overlooking a moonlit Lake Malaren. What could be more fun for a young girl in 1976 than being a Dancing Queen (yes, they did play it) in Stockholm, dancing away her cares with handsome blonde Bjorn and Benny lookalikes. I wanted the evening to never end; this was like a dream come true. I mean, all my travels were, but this was super-special. I'm not sure whether Zee and Chrissie had as much fun, although I think they did. I'm sure that being an Abba fan lent another dimension to my experiences of Stockholm. We all went back to the hotel tired and happy.

I remember waking during the night, the music from the evening before still going around in my head. It was so light outside, that I thought the time must be around six a.m. and I started to prepare for the new day. Then I looked at the clock radio and the dial said one a.m. I couldn't believe it, until I remembered the strange phenomenon of the Scandinavian countries: during summer, it's twilight all night and I guess in the winter, it's hardly ever twilight, but just dark.

Next day was Norway, which was beautiful too, but it was Sweden that won my heart and I've always wished for an opportunity to return. Unsurprisingly, I didn't ever run into any of the Abba members in Stockholm, but I attended their fantastic concert the following year, 1977, at the West Lakes Stadium. Abba were also frequently seen on ABC's *Countdown* in the mid to late 70s. I used to religiously watch the show every Sunday evening at six p.m.

40

And Then Back To London

I may have made you think that my Scandinavian tour stopped being fun and interesting after Stockholm. Not so! Certainly, I'd fallen in love with Sweden and wished for some more time there, but there was still delight to be had in Norway, Denmark (a different part of it this time) and northern Germany, in particular the fairy tale town of Hamelin, as in the Pied Piper, and the charm of Lübeck.

Sadly though, in Oslo, the man suffering from cancer died. All the tourists on our Globus bus were shocked and saddened, although we'd half expected it to happen. I don't think any of us had experienced a death on tour before. Luckily, it's a fairly rare occurrence. I recall that pompous old Gerald handled it pretty well and helped poor Mrs Dechant organise her sudden flight back to Quebec. I remember all of us taking her address, so that we could send her sympathy cards.

Oslo surprised me, but in a good way. It was much smaller than I'd imagined. By then, I was measuring just about every city against London or Stockholm. Oslo reminded me of Adelaide. There's a photo somewhere of a group of us sitting outside our hotel on a peaceful Sunday afternoon, during some downtime. It looks as if we're enjoying a coffee and just chatting. I'm wearing a red seersucker dress with coloured spots that my mum made for me. (Anyone remember seersucker?) I loved it and had several outfits made from this bumpy cotton material in my wardrobe. It struck me how quiet Oslo was on a Sunday afternoon, which again made me think of Adelaide back in 1976. I was proud of my red outfit as, despite the season being summer, the day was rather grey and overcast, so the splash of red stood out.

While in Oslo, we were taken to the Kon-Tiki Museum, where we saw Thor Heyerdahl's *Kon-Tiki* raft on which he sailed from South America to the Polynesian islands in the Pacific in 1947. There seemed to be hordes of people lined up to see it and progress around the raft was very slow, and the room was quite stuffy and warm. I found entertainment by catching the eye of a bloke across the other side, whereupon he tried to force his way through the people to join up with me. Stalker perhaps? It was a bit like a game of round and round the raft, instead of round and round the mulberry bush. I don't mean to make light of this exhibit; it was an incredible feat on the seemingly fragile craft, but rather him than me – Thor, I mean.

We spent a night in Lillehammer, a town I recall as being quite small, though very picturesque, with many of the buildings having whitewashed walls. It appeared sparklingly clean and glowed in the morning sunshine; summer flowers added splashes of colour – red, pink and purple everywhere. I'm sure it grew a lot between 1976 and 1994, which is when the little town hosted the Winter Olympics, but I can't help but wonder where they accommodated everyone. No doubt many private homeowners opened their doors.

One of the special purchases I made in Lillehammer was a gorgeous woollen jumper. It was cream with a red, black and green Nordic pattern on the front. There may have been some gold in there too. I took it proudly back home to Australia and wore it as often as possible. The timing was perfect, as I flew back into our winter. I always received compliments whenever I wore it and I still have it, though sadly it doesn't fit any more. I'd give it to my daughter who lives in Melbourne, where the weather is generally quite a bit chillier than Adelaide, but it's not her style. She's always scoffed at the idea of wearing jumpers; they belong in the wardrobes of mums and dads. Definitely not cool.

Many of Norway's fjords are, I believe, on their west coast, but we were taken to see one. Being summer there was no snow, but the scenery was breathtaking. On the day I saw it, the water was a sparkling bright blue, and the surrounding hills covered in pine forests, but having experienced European winters, I can easily visualise a landscape of icy blue, grey and white.

Northern Germany enchanted me and was like visiting a fairy tale. The more southern areas have Rothenburg on the Romantic Road and all the picture postcard towns along the Rhine, with their gingerbread-house-style of buildings along the river banks, but for me Lübeck was every bit as beautiful and seemed to shine in the sun. There were flowers everywhere and pleasantly warm sunshine, and locals outside to enjoy it.

However, you'll laugh when I relate to you one of the reasons why it was so memorable. One day, during a lunch stop, Zee and I found ourselves in a perfumery. I must admit, I'm unsure whether this was part of a chemist's shop (*Apotheke*) or was a specialty shop, but there was a promotion for the fragrance Givenchy Three. After the pretty blonde German girl who was promoting it sprayed us each in turn, I inhaled deeply and, being the spendthrift I was back then, decided I had to buy some. We both then waltzed out of the shop, smelling delicious, like the summer flowers in the town square. The short amount of time we had left was devoted to finding a café for coffee and cake, usually irresistible in Europe.

When packing later to return home, I put my precious bottle encased in its box into my hand luggage. However, the pressurisation on the flight that day caused a hole to blow out in the bottle and of course Givenchy Three was all over my hand luggage and it took months to get rid of the smell. Thank goodness I hadn't put it in my suitcase; fortunately, as an air hostess, I knew better than to put perfume into a suitcase. I liked Givenchy Three, but not that much.

In the early 90s, I again found myself enveloped in a cloud of Givenchy Three. I was working part-time doing Christmas promotions for the fragrance in David Jones. I faced stiff sales competition from girls promoting some of the newer fragrances on the market at that time, such as Tommy Hilfiger or Christian Dior's Poison, but I've always associated the classic Givenchy Three with Audrey Hepburn. At one time she used to be the face of Givenchy and you can't find a much better or more beautiful style icon that Audrey Hepburn.

Before I move on from Germany, I want to mention our visit to the East-West wall. I actually think this took place on our way to Scandinavia, but it's of historic significance and I didn't want to leave it out. We were on the Polish/German border. There were several guards, who looked benign enough, if a bit bored, although they had guns and I'm sure they'd have used them if they'd needed to. In 1976 the wall seemed destined to stay; no one ever thought that it would come down in 1989. It's a chilling reminder of the Cold War back then, and not unthinkable that it could happen again.

The last stop on our itinerary was Brussels, and I don't have a really clear memory of Brussels, other than that we were staying in the Ramada Inn on the Avenue Louise, one of the most elegant thoroughfares in the city. The lobby was chock-a-block with tourists, and many of the hotel staff seemed to be Spanish, but I saw enough to know that Brussels was worth another look further down the track. And it was to be in 1983 when John and I visited together and had a great time, except for the part where we got robbed (see 'Robbed in Brussels').

Zee and I spent some time walking along the Avenue Louise gazing at the exquisite lace shops and chocolate shops. At one of the haberdashery stores, I ventured inside and purchased (yes, of course I did) a really lovely combination of a collar and bodice in white lace. I'll turn it into a gorgeous dress sometime, I thought to myself. Little did I know then that it would form part of my wedding dress in 1980. I didn't have a wedding in mind when I bought it, just that it could be part of a formal outfit. I guess it became the 'something new' that all brides are supposed to have.

We also bought some chocolate, I think. Well, we must have, as you don't visit Brussels and not buy chocolate.

All too soon, the bus dropped us back at Ostend for the ferry ride back across to Dover and another hot crowded train. With so many memories, though, I didn't mind the train being uncomfortable.

A lace shop window in Brussels.

In London it was sad saying goodbyes to Chrissie and Zelma but, as I've said, they became long-term friends. I still keep in touch with Zee, but sadly Chrissie died at the end of the 90s.

For the last few days, I had a room in the London Hilton in Mayfair. It was very upmarket and had all the fancy facilities, but I didn't like the atmosphere. There were just too many rich, self-important people.

The day before I was to fly home, I had my suitcase and gear laid out on the bed to pack. I looked down into the park, which was called Green Park but now was more like Brown Park. The grass was so dry and England still hadn't had any rain in the two weeks I'd been out of the country. While packing, I had the radio on and I can clearly recall the hit songs being played: 'Don't Go Breaking My Heart' with Elton John and Kiki Dee, 'Sky Rockets in Flight, Afternoon Delight' by the Starland Vocal Band and 'Do Ya Think I'm Sexy?' by Rod Stewart.

'No, I don't, Rod,' I chuckled to myself.

Once again, Qantas delivered me home safely and in Australia I was greeted with green grass and rain; usually it's the other way around. You'll be glad to know that Ellen also made it home in one piece and didn't have any unpleasant encounters with axe-murderers, although she did sleep on a beach.

41

Grand Finale, Part 1

We know that all good things must come to an end, but sometimes we're just not ready for it. That's the way it happened for us at the end of our Britrail tour in 1983. It had been a five-week extravaganza of visiting different places, wonderful scenic railway journeys, and lots of delicious food – remember 'In Praise of Ploughman's Lunches and Peter Rabbit' and John's split trousers? Besides that, we met so many interesting people.

The thrills began on board our British 747 out of Melbourne. We had to touch down in Sydney first to pick up more people and as we were landing, we were nursing gin and tonics while gazing down at the Sydney Bridge and Harbour. The sound system was playing Elgar's 'Land of Hope and Glory'. You can't get more British than that.

I wasn't at all worried this time that John wasn't going to like London, as by now he'd been once and was as rapt as I was in all the possibilities it offered. Of course there was the hiccup with our Diners Club cards being stolen in Brussels (see 'Robbed in Brussels'), but we were, after a few days and a phone call on a very crackly phone line to the West Country, able to obtain new ones at the Diners Club office in St James Square. From there we took an evening train to York and our Britrail tour began for real.

The Britrail tour itself could almost cover another book, but here are some of the highlights. Walking around the York city wall offered fantastic views of the city and York Minster, plus the possibility of a fantastic fall just like Humpty Dumpty, if you happened to trip. In some places, the wall didn't have a barrier on both sides, so it was a bit

*Trains at Kings Cross Station, London.
One of them took us to Cambridge.*

The Roman wall in York.

scary. The Roman museum amazed us with its exhibits, of not only the Roman occupation of Britain, but the later Vikings as well. I've heard that even the street lay-out in York is based on the Viking grid. It was disappointing not being able to enter York Minster, which we'd so wanted to visit, but renovations were being carried out for the upcoming enthronement of the new archbishop of the time.

Following York, came Durham, where we were able to go into

that splendid cathedral. I was captivated by the early Christian history of not only the cathedral, which is the burial place for both Saint Cuthbert and the Venerable Bede, but I also loved the area in general; it is absolutely steeped in history. It being autumn, I'll always remember the colours of the trees along the riverbank on our way to the cathedral. Even the lady who ran the B&B where we stayed was memorable, if only for the funny little 'don't do this/don't do that' notes stuck on doors and walls everywhere.

Scotland was new to both of us and we started with Edinburgh where, because of a mix-up with our accommodation booking, the kind hosts gave us a super-huge room. It had obviously been part of a grand home once but was still beautifully maintained. We spent three wonderful cosy nights there in front of the heater, sipping our duty-free Scotch or cognac and discussing what we'd done that day. We toured Edinburgh Castle and Holyrood House, commonly called Holyrood Palace, where, we learned, Queen Elizabeth II stays. I loved the stories of intrigue and treachery involving Mary Queen of Scots and Elizabeth I. Wandering along the Royal Mile, we found some enticing shops. Calton Hill was fascinating too, as it was the remains of an ancient volcano. It was somehow weird to think of Scotland having volcanoes. We found a quaint little café where we enjoyed some of our meals. John had haggis

Edinburgh.

both times. Yes, really. He said I could have a taste, but I declined. I had been going to, but chickened out. I do remember their to-die-for ice cream sundaes, though. Oatcakes were something else we enjoyed for our Scottish breakfasts and we brought a box home to Australia with us.

Inverness was next and we had a bedroom with a beautiful view of distant snow-capped mountains. We had a lovely hostess there, Mrs Bailey. She was warm, welcoming and had a delightful accent. From Inverness we took a steam train ride over to the Isle of Skye. We just loved this three to four-hour trip, not only because of the steam train, but because it took us through very atmospheric, snowy, rather bleak Highland scenery. We were even buzzed by a low-flying RAF jet of the type being used in the Falklands War at the time. We enjoyed a fish and chip lunch in the crisp air outside, looking across to Skye with its crumbling old castle on the shores, which reminded us of a decayed tooth. We later took the ferry across to Skye – this was long before the bridge link was built – and meandered around. We even wandered into a pub with a view to having a drink, but a group of rather surly locals, while not quite hostile, but certainly not friendly, put us off. Still, we enjoyed our walk past the whitewashed crofters' cottages and loved the feeling of being so far north on the planet.

On our return train journey to Inverness, we struck up a lively conversation with two American girls. They were looking for somewhere to stay for the night.

'You must come with us,' I said. 'We're staying with a lovely person, and at the moment she has plenty of room.'

That morning at breakfast there had indeed only been me and John. When we arrived back, though, Mrs Bailey was booked out by three other couples who'd turned up while we were out. Being the off-season, it hadn't occurred to me that this might happen. I had egg on my face and felt very embarrassed. The two Americans were very nice about it, which didn't make me feel any better.

'That will teach me to open my big mouth,' I said to John.

The Lake District was next on the list, and I gave you a fairly detailed account of our time there in 'In Praise of Ploughman's Lunches and Peter Rabbit'. One funny incident I just want to relate quickly. The first B&B we booked into was considerably more expensive than some of the others but had only about half the space. Indeed, we had to clamber over the bed to get to the door. We'd booked several nights here, but we both agreed that we couldn't put up with such a tiny room that was costing so much more. Maybe it's an Aussie thing, needing lots of space. Next morning, we'd cooked up a story about having to leave earlier than we thought and needing to head back to London. A family drama, I think we said. The host was very sympathetic, which made us feel awful, as we'd really booked into another B&B just down the road, which was less expensive and, we hoped, roomier. We asked to book a taxi to take us to the railway station and nearly freaked out when the host offered to drive us there himself. We had no other choice but to accept. It was so embarrassing.

When we arrived at the station, we hopped out quickly, said our goodbyes and thank yous and promptly, as soon as the host had left, jumped into another cab to take us to the other B&B. We both ducked down as we drove past our original B&B. Goodness knows what the taxi driver thought of this pair of loony Aussies. Fortunately we didn't run into the former host and his wife over the next few days, although they could have seen us. Who knows?

After the Lake District was Chester. How we loved it. We stayed in a B&B within the old city walls. We somehow felt safe, although we certainly had no reason to feel unsafe. Perhaps hundreds of years ago people felt safe within the walls too. Although I guess it wasn't always enough to keep out marauders. Maybe just a psychological safe. Our B&B was opposite a Kings Head inn and we were intrigued to discover that all these Kings Head pubs/inns were havens sought by King Charles 1 when he was on the run for his life. A gay couple ran the B&B: Lillian and Jan and their two cute poodles. I only mention their being gay, as it was a more unusual situation, even in 1983, to find gay couples of either sex living openly together.

Ruins of a hypocaust in Chester. The other half lies under a convent.

Of course Chester has a wall too which you can walk around and, hip hooray, this one had a barrier on each side, so we, or at least I, felt more secure. We made a stop part way round to take a look at another Roman museum and one display I'll always remember was a Roman soldier's pay slip, with a deduction for the social club of the time. That seemed such a modern concept and it surprised me. As I've said before, sometimes it's just the little things that draw you in. Then, in a nearby park we came across an ancient Roman hypocaust, which had been part of a temple to the goddess Nemesis. Only half the temple was visible, the other half was lying under the next-door convent.

By then, it was December and Christmas decorations were arrayed across the main shopping thoroughfare. We loved the old wooden Tudor-type houses and we were sorry to move on, but we were looking forward to Wales. In northern Wales, we stayed in Betwys-y-Coed. We couldn't get over how beautiful northern Wales was and how cold. Our train from Chester took us via Birmingham, past Liverpool and also Conwy Castle. At the tiny little railway station of Betwys-y-Coed, we were met by Mr Pugh, who we'd phoned before leaving Chester. This was the famous journey where John's trousers split, because of our having enjoyed rather too many chips. Mr Pugh was a real character and had worked in Australia with ASIO for some years. His wife Dawn

Betwys-y-Coed.

was also Australian and she was delighted to welcome a couple of her fellow countrymen to their B&B.

The days that followed were some of the most relaxing of the whole trip. We went for walks, were buzzed by yet another RAF jet, enjoyed the crisp air, the forests and grey stone houses with their smoking chimneys. Swallow Falls were nearby, with plenty of water cascading over the rocks. So pretty. We also took a train/bus journey to Harlech Castle, which, built upon a massively steep rock, looked forbidding. Goodness knows what life must have been like in the fourteenth century when King Edward II was fighting for control of the castle. On the day we visited, we were the only two people there. John climbed up a stone staircase to the turrets and I stayed below and sat on what remained of one of the ancient walls, with a robin redbreast for company.

We were intrigued that sheep often used to wander up and down the Welsh railway platforms. This amused us. It looked as if they were awaiting a train to take them to town.

On the last night, we were treated to a special performance of Mr Pugh's Welsh choir, then went home and got warm by the heater guzzling Mr Pugh's Scotch, while he regaled us with some of his ASIO adventures. The Scotch loosened his tongue a fair bit, so we're not sure whether he repeated any classified information. After a very sound sleep, we awoke to be driven back to Betwys-y-Coed station en route to Hereford. Luckily, John's trousers remained intact this time.

The train trips from now on did not run as smoothly as on the east coast. There was more waiting around and changing trains. I remember a very long draughty wait on a freezing platform in Warrington, where we began to wonder if the trains were on strike. In Worcester, we had the pleasure of a ride in the guard's van with lots of others who, like us, were reluctant to share their carriage with a rowdy group of soccer hooligans. We made it to Hereford about seven p.m. and, having had nothing to eat since about ten that morning, went in search of some food, which is where we found a greasy spoon café and sneezing woman, a story I've already told in 'Sometimes It's Just the Little Things.'

In Hereford, there was so much to take pleasure in, including a visit to the cathedral and an afternoon service there. The cathedral was impressive both inside and out. A walk by the Wye River was tranquil and reflected clearly the nearby buildings, including the tower of the cathedral. Every time I have cider these days, I remember the Bulmer Cider brewery which we used to walk past on our way into the town. I also shouldn't forget the Hereford steak pies we ate in the Cathedral Café just before going to the service. There were many places where it would have been wonderful to have spent more time. After all, five weeks sounds a long time, but it was passing quickly and we wanted to fit in Bath before heading back to London.

We both absolutely adore Bath. We were there about three days and there's too much to write in this medley chapter. The Pump Room, where we enjoyed tea and bath buns, while listening to a Palm Court orchestra. Yes, I know it's touristy, but who cares. Bath Abbey, where Captain Arthur Phillip, a governor in the early days of New South Wales settlement, is buried. Some children were rehearsing for a nativity play there and they delivered their lines in a charming West Country accent: 'While shepherds were watching their flocks by night…'

The early-morning mist settled on the river and a golden sun shone

Jane Austen's former front door in Sydney Street, Bath.

through. We knocked on Jane Austen's door in Sydney Street: OK, we didn't knock of course, but I'm sure Jane Austen would have invited us in had she still been there and naturally we all would have liked each other immensely. I was reading one of her books during our longer train journeys. It was a selection of several stories, including *The Watsons*.

I mustn't forget the Roman baths, which, although unusable at the time we visited, had been renovated in the eighteenth century. A guard used to survey the activity in the pool and if he spotted any naughty goings-on, he'd wave a cane and call out, 'No hanky panky.'

We both developed colds in Bath, courtesy of Hereford's sneezing woman, and we were also getting a bit tired. Even thirty-somethings get tired after a while.

One thing I forgot to mention was during our substantial English

The Royal Crescent, Bath.

breakfasts, the host often had the telly turned on and *Good Morning Britain* was showing. This is how we first saw Boy George and his band playing their new hits 'Karma Chameleon' and 'Do You Really Want to Hurt Me?' Just a bit of historic trivia for you.

We caught a high-speed train back to Paddington Station and passed the time talking about all the things we wanted to do in London: A high tea at the Ritz or Savoy, communion in Westminster Abbey, some West End shows and Christmas shopping in Liberty, Selfridges and Marks and Spencer, and maybe the Scotch House if we had time. We anticipated having about ten more days before having to fly home. So much for our best-laid plans. Wait till I tell you in the next chapter how things actually played out. See what significant events occurred a few days after we'd left London.

42

Grand Finale, Part 2, With a Sting at the End of the Tale

We pulled into Paddington Station and took a black London cab – how we love those cabs – back to the Vicarage B&B in Kensington. It was almost like coming home, as on both holidays we'd stayed there and the area had became familiar to us. We enjoyed our walks down Kensington Church Street to Kensington High Street, where we'd catch a number 23 bus into London; or walking the other way, up to Bayswater Road, to catch a number 88 bus which took us to Westminster Abbey and the Houses of Parliament. We did do some of the special things we'd planned: communion in the abbey, an evening concert in John Smith Square, shopping at Liberty's again and morning tea in their tearoom, I think on the fourth floor. The fabric department in Liberty's was an almost overwhelming myriad of colour and choice, but I selected some lovely pieces to have made up by a dressmaker back in Adelaide. I remember John bought some shirt fabric lengths too, which he later had specially made. This was the next best thing to having them tailor made in Savile Row, but we, with a reasonable amount of disposable income, couldn't stretch to that, even in the 80s.

The weather was bitingly cold, though not snowy, and more than once we nearly skidded on the black ice hiding along the footpaths. It was also a good excuse to dive into warm pubs for more pub food; yes, chips again. We knew this habit would have to stop on our return home. The next four or five days went along pleasantly. We felt no need to rush and went into Leicester Square to buy tickets, for about four

The National Gallery, London.

days later, to see a Noel Coward play starring Penelope Keith. We fitted in some Christmas shopping and all seemed well.

One lunchtime however, I said to John, 'We'd better go to the British Airways office in Regent Street and check the loadings for our flight home.'

I'd probably better remind you here that we were both subject to load. I started to feel the slightest tinge of anxiety and this became a reality when, upon checking, the clerk in the BA office told us that the flights were chock-a-block full for the two weeks before Christmas and into the New Year. OMG (though we didn't use that phrase so much back then), we had completely underestimated the hordes of Brits visiting their relatives in Australia or just holidaying. How could we have been so stupid? BA told us to try Qantas or Singapore airlines. Qantas couldn't help us and, while Singapore Airlines said they had seats available, for some reason that I can't remember they couldn't swap our tickets over. This was a disaster. We knew we didn't have the funds to stay for another two weeks and, besides, I had to get back for work. Never again could I risk being back a day late for Airlines of South Australia.

What happened next was a lot of toing and froing between BA and the Singapore office. We cajoled and pleaded and still they wouldn't endorse our tickets over to another airline. John and I are not the sort of people who enjoy making a nuisance of ourselves. We are both by nature cooperative and courteous, but I knew that this was a battle we had to win; that we had to make ourselves nuisances and pests, and guess what? In the end, it paid off. To get us off their back, Singapore Airlines told us that they could accommodate us on a flight leaving Heathrow that evening – yes really, at seven p.m. – and if we could be there, they'd take us all the way to Melbourne. This was about four in the afternoon. We almost couldn't believe it. I think we offered our thanks profusely. We may have even knelt down and bowed three times to the east, but we had very hasty preparations to make if we wanted to get out of there before the Singapore Airlines staff decided that they hated us and changed their minds.

Outside in Regent Street it was starting to get dark, the Christmas decorations were lit up and the demand for late afternoon taxis was growing. We managed to hail one and, on the way back to the Vicarage, told the cabbie of our dilemma and asked him to please wait for us to pack and pay up the Vicarage staff. We paid him well to wait, then jumped out of the cab, and flew up the stairs to our room. It was nearly five p.m. by now. Can you imagine packing the contents of your travels from the past five and a half weeks, plus souvenirs and gifts, all in the space of about fifteen minutes? That's what we did, but we still had to get through evening traffic to Heathrow. We paid up, gave our Penelope Keith tickets to Mrs Divinney, the B&B manager, for either her or other guests to use, practically slid down the banisters, luggage and all, and out into the icy night for our race to Heathrow.

The cabbie, bless him, really put on the gas and despite evening London traffic deposited us safely to Terminal Three. We paid him, plus a sizeable tip. He wished us good luck and in we went to get boarding passes, hoping there wouldn't be any last-minute reversals of decisions. There wasn't, thank goodness, and we were driven down to the gate in one of those nifty little cars that staff zip around in to get from one section of the airport to another. I can't even remember going through customs or passport control. Needless to say, we were last to board. We only just made it. Our heads were still spinning, our pulses were absolutely racing, and the whole situation seemed surreal. We felt we were being spirited out of London.

Even when the plane took off, we couldn't quite take in all that was happening. We were leaving England, which we'd grown to love: the city, the museums, Kensington Gardens and Round Pond, the elegant shops, the red double-decker buses and the West End shows. Only days before we'd stood in Trafalgar Square, watching a promo being shot for *Singin' in the Rain*. Underneath our rapidly ascending plane, hidden by the darkness, was the gorgeous countryside, with its hedges, stiles and squirrels, and all the wonderful historic buildings. You name it. We were going to miss it terribly.

We couldn't totally relax on the journey back and almost expected to be offloaded in Singapore, where we wouldn't be certain how long it would take to return to Australia. Singapore Airlines have always been fairly generous in the complimentary drinks department and we made short work of whatever was offered.

We were finally flying over north-western Australia, the sun was rising and a clear summer sky greeted us as we lifted our sliding window blinds. The cabin smelled of fresh coffee. We were home and couldn't be offloaded now. I don't think any airline would drop off its passengers from a great height over Central Australia, do you?

About five days later – we'd left on a Monday evening in London – we heard on the news that Harrods had been bombed by the IRA. The bomb had been planted in a car down a side street. Six people were killed, three of them police officers and three civilians. Many more were injured. We were stunned, as we had planned to visit Harrods on that very day, around the same time, early afternoon. I had to do some checking on the net to remind myself of this. Was it why we'd been spirited out? Of course there's no way of knowing, but it was certainly an extraordinary coincidence.

We have never been able to go back to London. I left the airlines at the end of 1984. Once you leave, there are no more concessions, unless you're a captain; I have a feeling they continued to get airline concessions. I'll always feel grateful for what we had, though, and in writing these stories, have gained a new appreciation for all the fun and opportunities that I, then we, were able to experience. For those, I'm eternally thankful.

End of an era. My husband John came with me on my last flight, the Adelaide–Mt Gambier run. He was thrilled to be able to ride in the cockpit with the two pilots.

www.ingramcontent.com/pod-product-compliance
Lightning Source LLC
Chambersburg PA
CBHW070859080526
44589CB00013B/1133